2002 SUPPLEMENT

to

# CASES AND MATERIALS

ON

# EVIDENCE

NINTH EDITION

By

## JON R. WALTZ
Edna B. and Ednyfed H. Williams Professor of Law
and Lecturer in Medical Jurisprudence Emeritus
Northwestern University

## ROGER C. PARK
James Edgar Hervey Professor of Law
University of California
Hastings College of the Law

New York, New York
FOUNDATION PRESS
2002

COPYRIGHT © 2001 FOUNDATION PRESS
COPYRIGHT © 2002 By FOUNDATION PRESS
      395 Hudson Street
      New York, NY 10014
      Phone Toll Free 1–877–888–1330
      Fax (212) 367–6799
      fdpress.com

ISBN 1–58778–425–4

TEXT IS PRINTED ON 10% POST CONSUMER RECYCLED PAPER

# PREFACE

The purpose of this supplement is to bring the Ninth Edition of the Waltz & Park casebook up-to-date. We have tried to be concise. When in doubt, we have saved material for the next edition of the main volume rather than including it here.

We have included two Supreme Court cases that were decided since the main volume was published in 1999. In *Lilly v. Virginia*, 527 U.S. 116 (1999), the Court reversed a conviction on grounds that admission of an accomplice's statement under Virginia's hearsay exception for statements against penal interest violated the federal confrontation clause. In *Ohler v. United States*, 529 U.S. 753 (2001), the Court held that a criminal defense attorney's attempt to "remove the sting" by putting in evidence of prior convictions during the direct examination of the defendant forfeited the right to appeal the trial judge's prior decision that the convictions were admissible to impeach.

This supplement also contains the amendments to the Federal Rules of Evidence that became effective in December, 2000. These amendments codified the *Daubert* case, put restrictions on putting in hearsay through an expert witness, altered the language of Rule 701 to prevent expert testimony from sneaking in without notice under that rule, codified the forfeiture through misconduct hearsay doctrine, provided an alternative documentary foundation for business records, and provided that a party who loses a motion *in limine* need not raise the issue again at trial if the pretrial ruling was "definitive."

Finally, the supplement includes proposed amendments that are now in the process of being considered. The proposed amendment to Rule 608(b) would clarify the rule by stating expressly that the rule's extrinsic evidence ban applies to evidence about character for truthfulness. The proposed amendment to Rule 804(b)(3), the statement against interest exception, would extend the burden of corroboration to parties in civil cases and remind readers of the prosecution's burden to show trustworthiness under the Confrontation Clause.

JON R. WALTZ
ROGER C. PARK

June, 2002

# TABLE OF CONTENTS

[Insert at p. 347, before *Chambers v. Mississippi*]

## LILLY v. VIRGINIA

Supreme Court of the United States, 1999.
527 U.S. 116

Justice STEVENS announced the judgment of the Court and delivered the opinion of the Court with respect to Parts I, II, and VI, and an opinion with respect to Parts III, IV, and V, in which Justice SOUTER, Justice GINSBURG, and Justice BREYER join.

The question presented in this case is whether the accused's Sixth Amendment right "to be confronted with the witnesses against him" was violated by admitting into evidence at his trial a nontestifying accomplice's entire confession that contained some statements against the accomplice's penal interest and others that inculpated the accused.

### I   [6 Justices]

On December 4, 1995, three men--Benjamin Lee Lilly (petitioner), his brother Mark, and Mark's roommate, Gary Wayne Barker--broke into a home and stole nine bottles of liquor, three loaded guns, and a safe. The next day, the men drank the stolen liquor, robbed a small country store, and shot at geese with their stolen weapons. After their car broke down, they abducted Alex DeFilippis and used his vehicle to drive to a deserted location. One of them shot and killed DeFilippis. The three men then committed two more robberies before they were apprehended by the police late in the evening of December 5.

After taking them into custody, the police questioned each of the three men separately. Petitioner did not mention the murder to the police and stated that the other two men had forced him to participate in the robberies. Petitioner's brother Mark and Barker told the police somewhat different accounts of the crimes, but both maintained that petitioner masterminded the robberies and was the one who had killed DeFilippis.

A tape recording of Mark's initial oral statement indicates that he was questioned from 1:35 a.m. until 2:12 a.m. on December 6. The police interrogated him again from 2:30 a.m. until 2:53 a.m. During both interviews, Mark continually emphasized how drunk he had been during the entire spree. When asked about his participation in the string of crimes, Mark admitted that he stole liquor during the initial burglary and that he stole a 12-pack of beer during the robbery of the liquor store. Mark also conceded that he had handled a gun earlier that day and that he was present during the more serious thefts and the homicide.

The police told Mark that he would be charged with armed robbery and that, unless he broke "family ties," petitioner "may be dragging you right into a life sentence." Mark acknowledged that he would be sent away to the penitentiary. He claimed, however, that while he had primarily been drinking, petitioner and Barker had "got some guns or something" during the initial burglary. Mark said that Barker had pulled a gun in one of the robberies. He further insisted that petitioner had instigated the carjacking and that he (Mark) "didn't have nothing to do with the shooting" of DeFilippis. In a brief portion of one of his statements, Mark stated that petitioner was the one who shot DeFilippis.

The Commonwealth of Virginia charged petitioner with several offenses, including the murder of DeFilippis, and tried him separately. At trial, the Commonwealth called Mark as a witness, but he invoked his Fifth Amendment privilege against self-incrimination. The Commonwealth therefore offered to introduce into evidence the statements Mark made to the police after his arrest, arguing that they were admissible as declarations of an unavailable witness against penal interest. Petitioner objected on the ground that the statements were not actually against Mark's penal interest because they shifted responsibility for the crimes to Barker and to petitioner, and that their admission would violate the Sixth Amendment's Confrontation Clause. The trial judge overruled the objection and admitted the tape recordings and written transcripts of the statements in their entirety. The jury found petitioner guilty of robbery, abduction, carjacking, possession of a firearm by a felon, and four charges of illegal use of a firearm, for which offenses he received consecutive prison sentences of two life terms plus 27 years. The jury also convicted petitioner of capital murder and recommended a sentence of death, which the court imposed.

The Supreme Court of Virginia affirmed petitioner's convictions and sentences. As is relevant here, the court first concluded that Mark's statements were declarations of an unavailable witness against penal interest; that the statements' reliability was established by other evidence; and, therefore, that they fell within an exception to the Virginia hearsay rule. The court then turned to petitioner's Confrontation Clause challenge. It began by relying on our opinion in *White v. Illinois*, 502 U.S. 346 (1992), for the proposition that " '[w]here proffered hearsay has sufficient guarantees of reliability to come within a firmly rooted exception to the hearsay rule, the Confrontation Clause is satisfied.' " 499 S.E.2d 522, 534 (1998) (quoting *White*, 502 U.S., at 356). The Virginia court also remarked:

"[A]dmissiblity into evidence of the statement against penal interest of an unavailable witness is a 'firmly rooted' exception to the hearsay rule in Virginia. Thus, we hold that the trial court did not err in admitting Mark Lilly's statements into evidence." "That Mark Lilly's statements were self-serving, in that they tended to shift principal responsibility to others or to offer claims of mitigating circumstances, goes to the weight the jury could assign to them and not to their admissibility." 499 S.E.2d, at 534.

Our concern that this decision represented a significant departure from our Confrontation Clause jurisprudence prompted us to grant certiorari.

## II [5 Justices]

As an initial matter, the Commonwealth asserts that we should decline to exercise jurisdiction over petitioner's claim because he did not fairly present his Confrontation Clause challenge to the Supreme Court of Virginia. We disagree. Although petitioner focused on state hearsay law in his challenge to the admission of Mark's statements, petitioner expressly argued in his opening brief to that court that the admission of the statements violated his Sixth Amendment right to confrontation. He expanded his Sixth Amendment argument in his reply brief and cited *Lee v. Illinois*, 476 U.S. 530 (1986), and *Williamson v. United States*, 512 U.S. 594 (1994), in response to the Commonwealth's contention that the admission of the statements was constitutional. These arguments, particularly the reliance on our Confrontation Clause opinion in *Lee*, sufficed to raise in the Supreme Court of Virginia the constitutionality of admitting Mark's statements. See *Taylor v. Illinois*, 484 U.S. 400, 406, n.9 (1988). Indeed, the court addressed petitioner's Confrontation Clause claim without mentioning any waiver problems.

## III [4 Justices]

In all criminal prosecutions, state as well as federal, the accused has a right, guaranteed by the Sixth and Fourteenth Amendments to the United States Constitution, "to be confronted with the witnesses against him." U.S. Const., Amdt. 6; *Pointer v. Texas*, 380 U.S. 400 (1965) (applying Sixth Amendment to the States). "The central concern of the Confrontation Clause is to ensure the reliability of the evidence against a criminal defendant by subjecting it to rigorous testing in the context of an adversary proceeding before the trier of fact." *Maryland v. Craig*, 497 U.S. 836, 845 (1990). When the government seeks to offer a declarant's out-of-court statements against the accused, and, as in this case, the declarant is unavailable,[1] courts must decide whether the Clause permits the government to deny the accused his usual right to force the declarant "to submit to cross-examination, the 'greatest legal engine ever invented for the discovery of truth.'" *California v. Green*, 399 U.S. 149, 158 (1970) (footnote and citation omitted).

In our most recent case interpreting the Confrontation Clause, *White v. Illinois*, 502 U.S. 346 (1992), we rejected the suggestion that the Clause should be narrowly construed to apply only to practices comparable to "a particular abuse common in 16th- and 17th-century England: prosecuting a defendant through the presentation of *ex parte* affidavits, without the affiants ever being produced at trial." *Id.*, at 352. This abuse included using out-of-court depositions and "confessions of accomplices." *Green*, 399 U.S., at 157. Accord *White*, 502 U.S., at 361, 363 (noting that this rule applies even if the confession is "found to be reliable") (THOMAS, J., concurring in part and concurring in judgment). Because that restrictive reading of the Clause's term "witnesses" would have virtually eliminated the Clause's role in restricting the admission of hearsay testimony, we considered it foreclosed by our prior cases. Instead, we adhered to our general framework, summarized in *Ohio v. Roberts*, 448 U.S. 56 (1980), that the veracity of hearsay statements is sufficiently dependable to allow the untested admission of such statements against an accused when (1) "the evidence falls within a firmly rooted hearsay exception" or (2) it contains "particularized guarantees of trustworthiness" such that adversarial testing would be expected to add little, if anything, to the statements' reliability. *Id.*, at 66.

Before turning to the dual *Roberts* inquiries, however, we note that the statements taken from petitioner's brother in the early morning of December 6 were obviously obtained for the purpose of creating evidence that would be useful at a future trial. The analogy to the presentation of *ex parte* affidavits in the early English proceedings thus brings the Confrontation Clause into play no matter how narrowly its gateway might be read.

## IV [4 Justices]

The Supreme Court of Virginia held that the admission of Mark Lilly's confession was constitutional primarily because, in its view, it was against

---

[1]Petitioner suggests in his merits brief that Mark was not truly "unavailable" because the Commonwealth could have tried and sentenced him before petitioner's trial, thereby extinguishing Mark's Fifth Amendment privilege. We assume, however, as petitioner did in framing his petition for certiorari, that to the extent it is relevant, Mark was an unavailable witness for Confrontation Clause purposes.

Mark's penal interest and because "the statement against penal interest of an unavailable witness is a 'firmly rooted' exception to the hearsay rule in Virginia." 499 S.E.2d, at 534. We assume, as we must, that Mark's statements were against his penal interest as a matter of state law, but the question whether the statements fall within a firmly rooted hearsay exception for Confrontation Clause purposes is a question of federal law. Accordingly, it is appropriate to begin our analysis by examining the "firmly rooted" doctrine and the roots of the "against penal interest" exception.

We have allowed the admission of statements falling within a firmly rooted hearsay exception since the Court's recognition in *Mattox v. United States*, 156 U.S. 237 (1895), that the Framers of the Sixth Amendment "obviously intended to . . . respec[t]" certain unquestionable rules of evidence in drafting the Confrontation Clause. *Id.*, at 243. Justice Brown, writing for the Court in that case, did not question the wisdom of excluding deposition testimony, *ex parte* affidavits and their equivalents. But he reasoned that an unduly strict and "technical" reading of the Clause would have the effect of excluding other hearsay evidence, such as dying declarations, whose admissibility neither the Framers nor anyone else 100 years later "would have [had] the hardihood . . . to question." *Ibid.*

We now describe a hearsay exception as "firmly rooted" if, in light of "longstanding judicial and legislative experience," *Idaho v. Wright*, 497 U.S. 805, 817 (1990), it "rest[s][on] such [a] solid foundatio[n] that admission of virtually any evidence within [it] comports with the 'substance of the constitutional protection.'" *Roberts*, 448 U.S., at 66 (quoting *Mattox*, 156 U.S., at 244). This standard is designed to allow the introduction of statements falling within a category of hearsay whose conditions have proven over time "to remove all temptation to falsehood, and to enforce as strict an adherence to the truth as would the obligation of an oath" and cross-examination at a trial. *Mattox*, 156 U.S., at 244. In *White*, for instance, we held that the hearsay exception for spontaneous declarations is firmly rooted because it "is at least two centuries old," currently "widely accepted among the States," and carries "substantial guarantees of . . . trustworthiness . . . [that] cannot be recaptured even by later in-court testimony." 502 U.S., at 355-356, and n.8. Established practice, in short, must confirm that statements falling within a category of hearsay inherently "carr[y] special guarantees of credibility" essentially equivalent to, or greater than, those produced by the Constitution's preference for cross-examined trial testimony. *Id.*, at 356.

The "against penal interest" exception to the hearsay rule--unlike other previously recognized firmly rooted exceptions--is not generally based on the maxim that statements made without a motive to reflect on the legal consequences of one's statement, and in situations that are exceptionally conducive to veracity, lack the dangers of inaccuracy that typically accompany hearsay. The exception, rather, is founded on the broad assumption "that a person is unlikely to fabricate a statement against his own interest at the time it is made." *Chambers v. Mississippi*, 410 U.S. 284, 299 (1973).

We have previously noted that, due to the sweeping scope of the label, the simple categorization of a statement as a "'declaration against penal interest' . . . defines too large a class for meaningful Confrontation Clause analysis." *Lee v. Illinois*, 476 U.S., at 544, n.5. In criminal trials, statements against penal interest are offered into evidence in three principal situations: (1) as voluntary admissions against the declarant; (2) as exculpatory evidence offered by a defendant who claims that the declarant committed, or was involved in, the offense; and (3) as evidence offered by the prosecution to establish the guilt of an alleged accomplice of the declarant. It is useful to consider the three categories and their roots separately.

Statements in the first category--voluntary admissions of the declarant--are routinely offered into evidence against the maker of the statement and carry a distinguished heritage confirming their admissibility when so used. See G. Gilbert, Evidence 139-140 (1756); *Lambe's Case*, 2 Leach 552, 168 Eng. Rep. 379 (1791); *State v. Kirby*, 1 Strob. 155, 156 (1846); *State v. Cowan*, 29 N.C. 239, 246 (1847). Thus, assuming that Mark Lilly's statements were taken in conformance with constitutional prerequisites, they would unquestionably be admissible against him if he were on trial for stealing alcoholic beverages.

If Mark were a codefendant in a joint trial, however, even the use of his confession to prove his guilt might have an adverse impact on the rights of his accomplices. When dealing with admissions against penal interest, we have taken great care to separate using admissions against the declarant (the first category above) from using them against other criminal defendants (the third category).

In *Bruton v. United States*, 391 U.S. 123 (1968), two codefendants, Evans and Bruton, were tried jointly and convicted of armed postal robbery. A postal inspector testified that Evans had orally confessed that he and Bruton had committed the crime. The jury was instructed that Evans' confession was admissible against him, but could not be considered in assessing Bruton's guilt. Despite that instruction, this Court concluded that the introduction of Evans' confession posed such a serious threat to Bruton's right to confront and cross-examine the witnesses against him that he was entitled to a new trial. The case is relevant to the issue before us today, not because of its principal holding concerning the ability or inability of the jury to follow the judge's instruction, but rather because it was common ground among all of the Justices that the fact that the confession was a statement against the penal interest of Evans did not justify its use against Bruton. As Justice White noted at the outset of his dissent, "nothing in that confession which was relevant and material to Bruton's case was admissible against Bruton." *Id.*, at 138.

In the years since *Bruton* was decided, we have reviewed a number of cases in which one defendant's confession has been introduced into evidence in a joint trial pursuant to instructions that it could be used against him but not against his codefendant. Despite frequent disagreement over matters such as the adequacy of the trial judge's instructions, or the sufficiency of the redaction of ambiguous references to the declarant's accomplice, we have consistently either stated or assumed that the mere fact that one accomplice's confession qualified as a statement against his penal interest did not justify its use as evidence against another person. See *Gray v. Maryland*, 523 U.S. 185, 194-195 (1998) (stating that because the use of an accomplice's confession "creates a special, and vital, need for cross-examination," a prosecutor desiring to offer such evidence must comply with *Bruton*, hold separate trials, use separate juries, or abandon the use of the confession); *id.*, at 200 (SCALIA, J., dissenting) (stating that codefendant's confessions "may not be considered for the purpose of determining [the defendant's] guilt"); *Richardson v. Marsh*, 481 U.S. 200, 206 (1987) ("[W]here two defendants are tried jointly, the pretrial confession of one cannot be admitted against the other unless the confessing defendant takes the stand"); *Cruz v. New York*, 481 U.S. 186, 189-190, 193 (1987) (same).

The second category of statements against penal interest encompasses those offered as exculpatory evidence by a defendant who claims that it was the maker of the statement, rather than he, who committed (or was involved in) the crime in question. In this context, our Court, over the dissent of Justice Holmes, originally followed the 19th century English rule that categorically refused to recognize any "against penal interest" exception to the hearsay rule, holding instead that under federal law only hearsay statements against pecuniary (and perhaps proprietary) interest were sufficiently reliable to warrant their admission at the trial of someone other than the declarant. See *Donnelly v. United States*, 228 U.S. 243, 272-277 (1913). Indeed, most States adhered to this approach well into the latter half of the 20th century. See *Chambers*, 410 U.S., at 299 (collecting citations).

As time passed, however, the precise *Donnelly* rule, which barred the admission of other persons' confessions that exculpated the accused, became the subject of increasing criticism. Professor Wigmore, for example, remarked years after *Donnelly* that:

"The only practical consequences of this unreasoning limitation are shocking to the sense of justice; for, in its commonest application, it requires, in a criminal trial, the rejection of a confession, however well authenticated, of a person deceased or insane or fled from the jurisdiction (and therefore quite unavailable) who has avowed himself to be the true culprit . . . . It is therefore not too late to retrace our steps, and to discard this barbarous doctrine, which would refuse to let an innocent accused vindicate himself even by producing to the tribunal a perfectly authenticated written confession, made on the very gallows, by the true culprit now beyond the reach of justice." 5 J. Wigmore, Evidence § 1477, pp. 289-290 (3d ed.1940).

\* \* \*

Finally, in 1973, this Court endorsed the more enlightened view in *Chambers*, holding that the Due Process Clause affords criminal defendants the right to introduce into evidence third parties' declarations against penal interest--theirconfessions--when the circumstances surrounding the statements "provid[e] considerable assurance of their reliability." 410 U.S., at 300. Not surprisingly, most States have now amended their hearsay rules to allow the admission of such statements under against-penal-interest exceptions. \* \* \* But because hearsay statements of this sort are, by definition, offered by the accused, the admission of such statements does not implicate Confrontation Clause concerns. Thus, there is no need to decide whether the reliability of such statements is so inherently dependable that they would constitute a firmly rooted hearsay exception.

The third category includes cases, like the one before us today, in which the government seeks to introduce "a confession by an accomplice which incriminates a criminal defendant." *Lee*, 476 U.S., at 544, n.5. The practice of admitting statements in this category under an exception to the hearsay rule--to the extent that such a practice exists in certain jurisdictions--is, unlike the first category or even the second, of quite recent vintage. This category also typically includes statements that, when offered in the absence of the declarant, function similarly to those used in the ancient *ex parte* affidavit system.

Most important, this third category of hearsay encompasses statements that are inherently unreliable. Typical of the ground swell of scholarly and judicial criticism that culminated in the *Chambers* decision, Wigmore's treatise still expressly distinguishes accomplices' confessionsthat inculpate themselves and the accused as beyond a proper understanding of the against-penal-interest exception because an accomplice often has a considerable interest in "confessing and betraying his cocriminals." 5 Wigmore, Evidence § 1477, at

358, n.1. Consistent with this scholarship and the assumption that underlies the analysis in our *Bruton* line of cases, we have over the years "spoken with one voice in declaring presumptively unreliable accomplices' confessions that incriminate defendants." *Lee*, 476 U.S., at 541. See also *Cruz*, 481 U.S., at 195 (White, J., dissenting) (such statements "have traditionally been viewed with special suspicion"); *Bruton*, 391 U.S., at 136 (such statements are "inevitably suspect").

In *Crawford v. United States*, 212 U.S. 183 (1909), this Court stated that even when an alleged accomplice testifies, his confession that "incriminate[s] himself together with defendant . . . ought to be received with suspicion, and with the very greatest care and caution, and ought not to be passed upon by the jury under the same rules governing other and apparently credible witnesses." *Id.*, at 204. Over 30 years ago, we applied this principle to the Sixth Amendment. We held in *Douglas v. Alabama*, 380 U.S. 415 (1965), that the admission of a nontestifying accomplice's confession, which shifted responsibility and implicated the defendant as the triggerman, "plainly denied [the defendant] the right of cross-examination secured by the Confrontation Clause." *Id.*, at 419.

In *Lee*, we reaffirmed *Douglas* and explained that its holding "was premised on the basic understanding that when one person accuses another of a crime under circumstances in which the declarant stands to gain by inculpating another, the accusation is presumptively suspect and must be subjected to the scrutiny of cross-examination." 476 U.S., at 541. This is so because

> "th[e] truthfinding function of the Confrontation Clause is uniquely threatened when an accomplice's confession is sought to be introduced against a criminal defendant without the benefit of cross-examination . . . . 'Due to his strong motivation to implicate the defendant and to exonerate himself, a codefendant's statements about what the defendant said or did are less credible than ordinary hearsay evidence.'" *Ibid.* (quoting *Bruton*, 391 U.S., at 141 (White, J., dissenting)).

Indeed, even the dissenting Justices in *Lee* agreed that "accomplice confessions ordinarily are untrustworthy precisely because they are *not* unambiguously adverse to the penal interest of the declarant" but instead are likely to be attempts to minimize the declarant's culpability. 476 U.S., at 552-553 (Blackmun, J., dissenting).[2]

_____

[2]The only arguable exception to this unbroken line of cases arose in our plurality opinion in *Dutton v. Evans*, 400 U.S. 74 (1970), in which we held that the admission of an accomplice's spontaneous comment that indirectly inculpated the defendant did not violate the Confrontation Clause. While Justice Stewart's lead opinion observed

10

We have adhered to this approach in construing the Federal Rules of Evidence. Thus, in *Williamson v. United States*, 512 U.S. 594 (1994), without reaching the Confrontation Clause issue, we held that an accomplice's statement against his own penal interest was not admissible against the defendant.[3] We once again noted the presumptive unreliability of the "non-self-inculpatory" portions of the statement: "One of the most effective ways to lie is to mix falsehood with truth, especially truth that seems particularly persuasive because of its self-inculpatory nature." *Id.*, at 599-601.

It is clear that our cases consistently have viewed an accomplice's statements that shift or spread the blame to a criminal defendant as falling outside the realm of those "hearsay exception[s] [that are] so trustworthy that adversarial testing can be expected to add little to [the statements'] reliability." *White*, 502 U.S., at 357. This view is also reflected in several States' hearsay law.[4] Indeed, prior to 1995, it appears that even Virginia rarely allowed

---

that the declarant's statement was "against his penal interest," *id.*, at 89, the Court's judgment did not rest on that point, and in no way purported to hold that statements with such an attribute were presumptively admissible. Rather, the five Justices in the majority emphasized the unique aspects of the case and emphasized that the coconspirator spontaneously made the statement and "had no apparent reason to lie." *Id.*, at 86-89. See also *id.*, at 98 (Harlan, J., concurring in result).

[3]Federal Rule of Evidence 804(b)(3) provides an exception to the hearsay rule for the admission of "[a] statement which was at the time of its making so far contrary to the declarant's pecuniary or proprietary interest, or so far tended to subject the declarant to civil or criminal liability . . . that a reasonable person in the declarant's position would not have made the statement unless believing it to be true."

[4]Several States provide statutorily that their against-penal-interest hearsay exceptions do not allow the admission of "[a] statement or confession offered against the accused in a criminal case, made by a codefendant or other person implicating both himself and the accused." Ark. Rule Evid. 804(b)(3) (1997). Accord, Ind. Rule Evid. 803(b)(3) (1999); Me. Rule Evid. 804(b)(3) (1998); Nev. Rev. Stat. § 51.345(2) (Supp.1996); N.J. Rule Evid. 803(25)(c) (1999); N.D. Cent. Code Rule Evid. § 804(b)(3) (1998); Vt. Rule Evid. 804(b)(3) (1998). See also *State v. Myers*, 229 Kan.168, 172-173, 625 P.2d 1111, 1115 (1981) ("Under 60-460(*f*), a hearsay confession of one coparticipant in a crime is not admissible against *another coparticipant*" ). Several other States have adopted the language of the Federal Rule, see n.3, *supra*, and adhere to our interpretation of that rule in *Williamson*. See *Smith v. State*, 647 A.2d 1083, 1088 (Del.1994); *United States v. Hammond*, 681 A.2d 1140, 1146 (Ct. App. D.C. 1996); *State v. Smith*, 643 So.2d 1221, 1221- 1222 (La.1994); *State v. Matusky*, 343 Md. 467, 490-492, and n.15, 682 A.2d 694, 705-706, and n.15 (1996); *State v. Ford*, 539 N.W.2d 214, 227 (Minn.1995); *State v. Castle*, 285 Mont. 363, 373-374, 948 P.2d 688, 694

statements against the penal interest of the declarant to be used at criminal trials. See, *e.g., Ellison v. Commonwealth,* 247 S.E.2d 685 (1978). That Virginia relaxed that portion of its hearsay law when it decided *Chandler v. Commonwealth,* 455 S.E.2d 219 (1995), and that it later apparently concluded that all statements against penal interest fall within "a 'firmly rooted' exception to the hearsay rule in Virginia," 499 S.E.2d, at 534, is of no consequence. The decisive fact, which we make explicit today, is that accomplices' confessions that inculpate a criminal defendant are not within a firmly rooted exception to the hearsay rule as that concept has been defined in our Confrontation Clause jurisprudence.[5]

---

(1997); *Miles v. State,* 918 S.W.2d 511, 515 (Tex. Ct. Crim. App.1996); *In re Anthony Ray, Mc.,* 200 W. Va. 312, 321, 489 S.E.2d 289, 298 (1997). Still other States have virtually no against-penal-interest exception at all. See Ala. Rule Evid. 804(b)(3) (1998) (no such exception); Ga. Code Ann. § 24-3-8 (1995) (exception only if declarant is deceased and statement was not made with view toward litigation); *State v. Skillicorn,* 944 S.W.2d 877, 884-885(Mo.) (no exception), cert. denied, 522 U.S. 999 (1997).

[5]Our holdings in *Bruton v. United States,* 391 U.S. 123 (1968), *Cruz v. New York,* 481 U.S. 186 (1987), *Gray v. Maryland,* 523 U.S. 185 (1998), and *Lee v. Illinois,* 476 U.S. 530 (1986), were all premised, explicitly or implicitly, on the principle that accomplice confessions that inculpate a criminal defendant are not *per se* admissible (and thus necessarily fall outside a firmly rooted hearsay exception), no matter how much those statements also incriminate the accomplice. If "genuinely" or "equally" inculpatory confessions of accomplices were--as THE CHIEF JUSTICE's concurrence suggests is possible, *post,* at 1904-1905--*per se* admissible against criminal defendants, then the confessions in each of those cases would have been admissible, for each confession inculpated the accomplice equally in the crimes at issue. But the Court in *Lee* rejected the dissent's position that nontestifying accomplice's confessions that are "unambiguously" against the accomplice's penal interest are *per se* admissible, see 476 U.S., at 552 (Blackmun, J., dissenting) and we ruled in *Bruton, Cruz,* and *Gray* that such equally self-inculpatory statements are inadmissible against criminal defendants. Today we merely reaffirm these holdings and make explicit what was heretofore implicit: A statement (like Mark's) that falls into the category summarized in *Lee*--"a confession by an accomplice which incriminates a criminal defendant," 476 U.S., at 544, n.5--does not come within a firmly rooted hearsay exception.

This, of course, does not mean, as THE CHIEF JUSTICE and Justice THOMAS erroneously suggest, see *post,* at 1905, and *post,* at 1903-1904, that the Confrontation Clause imposes a "blanket ban on the government's use of [nontestifying] accomplice statements that incriminate a defendant." Rather, it simply means that the Government must satisfy the second prong of the *Ohio v. Roberts,* 448 U.S. 56 (1980), test in order to introduce such statements. See Part V, *infra.*

12

## V [4 Justices]

Aside from its conclusion that Mark's statements were admissible under a firmly rooted hearsay exception, the Supreme Court of Virginia also affirmed the trial court's holding that the statements were "reliabl[e] . . . in the context of the facts and circumstances under which [they were] given" because (I) "Mark Lilly was cognizant of the import of his statements and that he was implicating himself as a participant in numerous crimes" and (ii) "[e]lements of [his] statements were independently corroborated" by other evidence offered at trial. 499 S.E.2d, at 534. The Commonwealth contends that we should defer to this "fact-intensive" determination. It further argues that these two indicia of reliability, coupled with the facts that the police read Mark his *Miranda* rights and did not promise him leniency in exchange for his statements, demonstrate that the circumstances surrounding his statements bore "particularized guarantees of trustworthiness," *Roberts*, 448 U.S., at 66, sufficient to satisfy the Confrontation Clause's residual admissibility test.[6]

The residual "trustworthiness" test credits the axiom that a rigid application of the Clause's standard for admissibility might in an exceptional case exclude a statement of an unavailable witness that is incontestably probative, competent, and reliable, yet nonetheless outside of any firmly rooted hearsay exception. Cf. *id.*, at 63; *Mattox*, 156 U.S., at 243-244. When a court can be confident--as in the context of hearsay falling within a firmly rooted exception--that "the declarant's truthfulness is so clear from the surrounding circumstances that the test of cross-examination would be of marginal utility," the Sixth Amendment's residual "trustworthiness" test allows the admission of the declarant's statements. *Wright*, 497 U.S., at 820.

Nothing in our prior opinions, however, suggests that appellate courts should defer to lower courts' determinations regarding whether a hearsay statement has particularized guarantees of trustworthiness. To the contrary, those opinions indicate that we have assumed, as with other fact-intensive,

---

[6]Although THE CHIEF JUSTICE contends that we should remand this issue to the Supreme Court of Virginia, see *post*, at 1905-1906, it would be inappropriate to do so because we granted certiorari on this issue, and the parties have fully briefed and argued the issue. The "facts and circumstances" formula, recited above, that the Virginia courts already employed in reaching their reliability holdings is virtually identical to the *Roberts* "particularized guarantees" test, which turns as well on the "surrounding circumstances" of the statements. *Idaho v. Wright*, 497 U.S. 805, 820 (1990). Furthermore, as will become clear, the Commonwealth fails to point to any fact regarding this issue that the Supreme Court of Virginia did not explicitly consider and that requires serious analysis.

mixed questions of constitutional law, that "independent review is . . . necessary . . . to maintain control of, and to clarify, the legal principles" governing the factual circumstances necessary to satisfy the protections of the Bill of Rights. *Ornelas v. United States*, 517 U.S. 690, 697 (1996) (holding that appellate courts should review reasonable suspicion and probable cause determinations *de* novo). We, of course, accept the Virginia courts' determination that Mark's statements were reliable for purposes of state hearsay law, and, as should any appellate court, we review the presence or absence of historical facts for clear error. But the surrounding circumstances relevant to a Sixth Amendment admissibility determination do not include the declarant's in-court demeanor (otherwise the declarant would be testifying) or any other factor uniquely suited to the province of trial courts. For these reasons, when deciding whether the admission of a declarant's out-of-court statements violates the Confrontation Clause, courts should independently review whether the government's proffered guarantees of trustworthiness satisfy the demands of the Clause.

The Commonwealth correctly notes that "the presumption of unreliability that attaches to codefendants' confessions . . . may be rebutted." *Lee*, 476 U.S., at 543. We have held, in fact, that any inherent unreliability that accompanies co-conspirator statements made during the course and in furtherance of the conspiracy is *per se* rebutted by the circumstances giving rise to the long history of admitting such statements. See *Bourjaily v. United States*, 483 U.S. 171, 182-184 (1987). Nonetheless, the historical underpinnings of the Confrontation Clause and the sweep of our prior confrontation cases offer one cogent reminder: It is highly unlikely that the presumptive unreliability that attaches to accomplices' confessions that shift or spread blame can be effectively rebutted when the statements are given under conditions that implicate the core concerns of the old *ex parte* affidavit practice--that is, when the government is involved in the statements' production, and when the statements describe past events and have not been subjected to adversarial testing.

Applying these principles, the Commonwealth's asserted guarantees of trustworthiness fail to convince us that Mark's confession was sufficiently reliable as to be admissible without allowing petitioner to cross-examine him. That other evidence at trial corroborated portions of Mark's statements is irrelevant. We have squarely rejected the notion that "evidence corroborating the truth of a hearsay statement may properly support a finding that the statement bears 'particularized guarantees of trustworthiness.'" *Wright*, 497 U.S., at 822. In *Wright*, we concluded that the admission of hearsay statements by a child declarant violated the Confrontation Clause even though the statements were admissible under an exception to the hearsay rule recognized in Idaho, and even though they were corroborated by other evidence. We recognized that it was theoretically possible for such statements to possess "'particularized guarantees of trustworthiness'" that would justify their admissibility, but we refused to allow the State to "bootstrap on" the trustworthiness of other evidence. "To be admissible under the Confrontation Clause," we held, "hearsay evidence used to convict a defendant must possess indicia of reliability by virtue of its inherent trustworthiness, not by reference to other evidence at trial." *Ibid.*

Nor did the police's informing Mark of his *Miranda* rights render the circumstances surrounding his statements significantly more trustworthy. We noted in rejecting a similar argument in *Lee* that a finding that a confession was "voluntary for Fifth Amendment purposes . . . does not bear on the question of whether the confession was also free from any desire, motive, or impulse [the declarant] may have had either to mitigate the appearance of his own culpability by spreading the blame or to overstate [the defendant's] involvement" in the crimes at issue. 476 U.S., at 544. By the same token, we believe that a suspect's consciousness of his *Miranda* rights has little, if any, bearing on the likelihood of truthfulness of his statements. When a suspect is in custody for his obvious involvement in serious crimes, his knowledge that anything he says may be used against him militates against depending on his veracity.

The Commonwealth's next proffered basis for reliability--that Mark knew he was exposing himself to criminal liability--merely restates the fact that portions of his statements were technically against penal interest. And as we have explained, such statements are suspect insofar as they inculpate other persons. "[T]hat a person is making a broadly self-inculpatory confession does not make more credible the confession's non-self-inculpatory parts." *Williamson*, 512 U.S., at 599. Accord, *Lee*, 476 U.S., at 545. Similarly, the absence of an express promise of leniency to Mark does not enhance his statements' reliability to the level necessary for their untested admission. The police need not tell a person who is in custody that his statements may gain him leniency in order for the suspect to surmise that speaking up, and particularly placing blame on his cohorts, may inure to his advantage.

It is abundantly clear that neither the words that Mark spoke nor the setting in which he was questioned provides any basis for concluding that his comments regarding petitioner's guilt were so reliable that there was no need to subject them to adversarial testing in a trial setting. Mark was in custody for his involvement in, and knowledge of, serious crimes and made his statements under the supervision of governmental authorities. He was primarily responding to the officers' leading questions, which were asked without any contemporaneous cross-examination by adverse parties. Thus, Mark had a natural motive to attempt to exculpate himself as much as possible. See *id.*, at 544-545; *Dutton v. Evans*, 400 U.S. 74, 98 (1970) (HARLAN, J., concurring in result). Mark also was obviously still under the influence of alcohol. Each of these factors militates against finding that his statements were so inherently reliable that cross-examination would have been superfluous.

## VI [6 Justices]

The admission of the untested confession of Mark Lilly violated petitioner's Confrontation Clause rights. Adhering to our general custom of allowing state courts initially to assess the effect of erroneously admitted evidence in light of substantive state criminal law, we leave it to the Virginia courts to consider in the first instance whether this Sixth Amendment error was "harmless beyond a reasonable doubt." *Chapman v. California*, 386 U.S. 18, 24 (1967). See also *Lee*, 476 U.S., at 547. Accordingly, the judgment of the Supreme Court of Virginia is reversed, and the case is remanded for further proceedings not inconsistent with this opinion.

*It is so ordered.*

Justice BREYER, concurring.

As currently interpreted, the Confrontation Clause generally forbids the introduction of hearsay into a trial unless the evidence "falls within a firmly rooted hearsay exception" or otherwise possesses "particularized guarantees of trustworthiness." *Ohio v. Roberts*, 448 U.S. 56, 66 (1980). *Amici* in this case, citing opinions of Justices of this Court and the work of scholars, have argued that we should reexamine the way in which our cases have connected the Confrontation Clause and the hearsay rule. See Brief for American Civil Liberties Union et al. as *Amici Curiae* 2-3; see also, *e.g., White v. Illinois*, 502 U.S. 346, 358 (1992) (THOMAS, J., joined by SCALIA, J., concurring in part and concurring in judgment); Friedman, Confrontation: The Search for Basic Principles, 86 Geo. L.J. 1011 (1998); A. Amar, The Constitution and Criminal Procedure 129 (1997); Berger, The Deconstitutionalization of the Confrontation Clause: A Proposal for a Prosecutorial Restraint Model, 76 Minn. L. Rev. 557 (1992).

The Court's effort to tie the Clause so directly to the hearsay rule is of fairly recent vintage, compare *Roberts, supra,* with *California v. Green*, 399 U.S. 149, 155-156 (1970), while the Confrontation Clause itself has ancient origins that predate the hearsay rule, see *Salinger v. United States*, 272 U.S. 542, 548 (1926) ("The right of confrontation did not originate with the provision in the Sixth Amendment, but was a common-law right having recognized exceptions"). The right of an accused to meet his accusers face-to-face is mentioned in, among other things, the Bible, Shakespeare, and 16th and 17th century British statutes, cases, and treatises. See The Bible, Acts 25:16; W. Shakespeare, Richard II, act I, sc. 1; W. Shakespeare, Henry VIII, act ii, sc. 1; 30 Charles A. Wright & Kenneth W. Graham, Federal Practice and Procedure § 6342, p. 227 (1997) (quoting statutes enacted under King Edward VI in 1552 and Queen Elizabeth I in 1558); cf. Case of Thomas Tong, Kelyng J. 17, 18, 84 Eng. Rep. 1061, 1062 (1662) (out-of-court confession may be used against the confessor, but not against his co-conspirators); M. Hale, History of the Common Law of England 163-164 (C. Gray ed.1971); 3 W. Blackstone, Commentaries *373. As traditionally understood, the right was designed to prevent, for example, the kind of abuse that permitted the Crown to convict Sir Walter Raleigh of treason on the basis of the out-of-court confession of Lord Cobham, a co-conspirator. See 30 Wright & Graham, *supra*, § 6342, at 258-269.

Viewed in light of its traditional purposes, the current, hearsay-based Confrontation Clause test, *amici* argue, is both too narrow and too broad. The test is arguably too narrow insofar as it authorizes the admission of out-of-court statements prepared as testimony for a trial when such statements happen to fall within some well-recognized hearsay rule exception. For example, a deposition or videotaped confession sometimes could fall within the exception for vicarious admissions or, in THE CHIEF JUSTICE's view, the exception for statements against penal interest. See *post*, at 1904-1905. See generally *White, supra*, at 364-365 (THOMAS, J., concurring in part and concurring in judgment); Friedman, *supra*, at 1025; Amar, *supra*, at 129; Berger, *supra*, at 596-602; Brief for the American Civil Liberties Union et al. as *Amici Curiae* 16-20. But why should a modern Lord Cobham's out-of-court confession become admissible simply because of a fortuity, such as the conspiracy having continued through the time of police questioning, thereby bringing the confession within the "well-established" exception for the vicarious admissions of a co-conspirator? Cf. *Dutton v. Evans*, 400 U.S. 74, 83 (1970) (plurality opinion). Or why should we, like Walter Raleigh's prosecutor, deny a plea to "let my Accuser come face to face," with words (now related to the penal interest exception) such as, "The law presumes, a man will not accuse himself to accuse another"? *Trial of Sir Walter Raleigh*, 2 How. St. Tr. 19 (1816).

At the same time, the current hearsay-based Confrontation Clause test is arguably too broad. It would make a constitutional issue out of the admission of *any* relevant hearsay statement, even if that hearsay statement is only tangentially related to the elements in dispute, or was made long before the crime occurred and without relation to the prospect of a future trial. It is not obvious that admission of a business record, which is hearsay because the business was not "regularly conducted," or admission of a scrawled note,

"Mary called," dated many months before the crime, violates the defendant's basic *constitutional* right "to be confronted with the witnesses against him." Yet one cannot easily fit such evidence within a traditional hearsay exception. Nor can one fit it within this Court's special exception for hearsay with "particularized guarantees of trustworthiness"; and, in any event, it is debatable whether the Sixth Amendment principally protects "trustworthiness," rather than "confrontation." See *White, supra,* at 363 (THOMAS, J., concurring in part and concurring in judgment); cf. *Maryland v. Craig,* 497 U.S. 836, 862 (1990) (SCALIA, J., dissenting) ("[T]he Confrontation Clause does not guarantee reliable evidence; it guarantees specific trial procedures that were thought to *assure* reliable evidence, undeniably among which was 'face-to-face' confrontation").

We need not reexamine the current connection between the Confrontation Clause and the hearsay rule in this case, however, because the statements at issue violate the Clause regardless. See *ante,* at 125. I write separately to point out that the fact that we do not reevaluate the link in this case does not end the matter. It may leave the question open for another day.

Justice SCALIA, concurring in part and concurring in the judgment.

During a custodial interrogation, Mark Lilly told police officers that petitioner committed the charged murder. The prosecution introduced a tape recording of these statements at trial without making Mark available for cross-examination. In my view, that is a paradigmatic Confrontation Clause violation. See *White v. Illinois,* 502 U.S. 346, 364-365 (1992) (THOMAS, J., concurring in part and concurring in judgment) ("The federal constitutional right of confrontation extends to any witness who actually testifies at trial" and "extrajudicial statements only insofar as they are contained in formalized testimonial material, such as affidavits, depositions, prior testimony, or confessions"). Since the violation is clear, the case need be remanded only for a harmless-error determination. I therefore join Parts I, II, and VI of the Court's opinion and concur in the judgment.

Justice THOMAS, concurring in part and concurring in the judgment.

I join Parts I and VI of the Court's opinion and concur in the judgment. Though I continue to adhere to my view that the Confrontation Clause "extends to any witness who actually testifies at trial" and "is implicated by extrajudicial statements only insofar as they are contained in formalized testimonial material, such as affidavits, depositions, prior testimony, or confessions," *White v. Illinois,* 502 U.S. 346, 365 (1992) (opinion concurring in part and concurring in judgment), I agree with THE CHIEF JUSTICE that the Clause does not impose a "blanket ban on the government's use of accomplice statements that incriminate a defendant." *Post,* at 147. Such an approach not only departs from an original understanding of the Confrontation Clause but also freezes our jurisprudence by making trial court decisions excluding such statements virtually unreviewable. I also agree with THE CHIEF JUSTICE that the lower courts did not "analyz[e] the confession under the second prong of the *Roberts* inquiry," *post*, at 148, and therefore see no reason for the plurality to address an issue upon which those courts did not pass.

Chief Justice REHNQUIST, with whom Justice O'CONNOR and Justice KENNEDY join, concurring in the judgment.

The plurality today concludes that all accomplice confessions that inculpate a criminal defendant are not within a firmly rooted exception to the hearsay rule under *Ohio v. Roberts*, 448 U.S. 56 (1980). See *ante*, at 134. It also concludes that appellate courts should independently review the government's proffered guarantees of trustworthiness under the second half of the *Roberts* inquiry. See *ante*, at 135. I disagree with both of these conclusions, but concur in the judgment reversing the decision of the Supreme Court of Virginia.

I

The plurality correctly states the issue in this case in the opening sentence of its opinion: Whether petitioner's Confrontation Clause rights were violated by admission of an accomplice's confession "that contained some statements against the accomplice's penal interest and others that inculpated the accused." *Ante*, at [1]. The confession of the accomplice, Mark Lilly, covers 50 pages in the Joint Appendix, and the interviews themselves lasted about an hour. The statements of Mark Lilly which are against his penal interest--and would probably show him as an aider and abettor--are quite separate in time and place from other statements exculpating Mark and incriminating his brother, petitioner Benjamin Lilly, in the murder of Alexis DeFilippis.[1]

---

[1]Mark identifies Ben as the one who murdered Alexis DeFilippis in the following colloquy:

> "M. L.: I don't know, you know, dude shoots him.
> "G. P.: When you say 'dude shoots him' which one are you calling a dude here?
> "M. L.: Well, Ben shoots him.
> "G. P.: Talking about your brother, what did he shoot him with?
> "M. L.: Pistol.
> "G. P.: How many times did he shoot him?
> "M. L.: I heard a couple of shots go off, I don't know how many times he hit him." App. 258.

A similar colloquy occurred in the second interview. See *id.*, at 312-313.

Thus one is at a loss to know why so much of the plurality's opinion is devoted to whether a declaration against penal interest is a "firmly rooted exception" to the hearsay rule under *Ohio v. Roberts, supra*. Certainly, we must accept the Virginia court's determination that Mark's statements as a whole were declarations against penal interest for purposes of the Commonwealth's hearsay rule. Simply labeling a confession a "declaration against penal interest," however, is insufficient for purposes of *Roberts*, as this exception "defines too large a class for meaningful Confrontation Clause analysis." *Lee v. Illinois*, 476 U.S. 530, 544, n.5 (1986). The plurality tries its hand at systematizing this class, but most of its housecleaning is unwarranted and results in a complete ban on the government's use of accomplice confessions that inculpate a codefendant. Such a categorical holding has no place in this case because the relevant portions of Mark Lilly's confession were simply not "declarations against penal interest" as that term is understood in the law of evidence. There may be close cases where the declaration against penal interest portion is closely tied in with the portion incriminating the defendant, see 2 J. Strong, McCormick on Evidence § 319 (4th ed.1992), but this is not one of them. Mark Lilly's statements inculpating his brother in the murder of DeFilippis are not in the least against Mark's penal interest.

This case therefore does not raise the question whether the Confrontation Clause permits the admission of a genuinely self-inculpatory statement that also inculpates a codefendant, and our precedent does not compel the broad holding suggested by the plurality today. Cf. *Williamson v. United States*, 512 U.S. 594, 618-619 (1994) (KENNEDY, J. concurring) (explaining and providing examples of self-serving and more neutral declarations against penal interest). Indeed, several Courts of Appeals have admitted custodial confessions that equally inculpate both the declarant and the defendant, [2] and I see no reason for us to preclude consideration of these or similar statements as satisfying a firmly rooted hearsay exception under *Roberts*.

Not only were the incriminating portions of Mark Lilly's confession not a declaration against penal interest, but these statements were part of a custodial confession of the sort that this Court has viewed with "special suspicion" given a codefendant's "'strong motivation to implicate the defendant and to

---

[2]See, *e.g.*, *United States v. Keltner*, 147 F.3d 662, 670 (CA8 1998) (statement "clearly subjected" declarant to criminal liability for "activity in which [he] participated and was planning to participate with . . . both defendants"); *Earnest v. Dorsey*, 87 F.3d 1123, 1134 (CA10 1996) ("entire statement inculpated both [defendant]and [declarant] equally" and "neither [attempted] to shift blame to his co- conspirators nor to curry favor from the police or prosecutor").

exonerate himself.'" *Lee, supra*, at 541 (citations omitted). Each of the cases cited by the plurality to support its broad conclusion involved accusatory statements taken by law enforcement personnel with a view to prosecution. See *Douglas v. Alabama*, 380 U.S. 415, 416-417 (1965); *Lee, supra*, 532-536; cf. *Bruton v. United States*, 391 U.S. 123, 124-125 (1968); *Williamson, supra*, at 596-597. These cases did not turn solely on the fact that the challenged statement inculpated the defendant, but were instead grounded in the Court's suspicion of untested custodial confessions. See, *e.g., Lee, supra*, at 544-545. The plurality describes *Dutton v. Evans*, 400 U.S. 74 (1970), as an "exception" to this line of cases, *ante*, at 132, n.2, but that case involved an accomplice's statement to a fellow prisoner, see 400 U.S., at 77-78, not a custodial confession.

The Court in *Dutton* held that the admission of an accomplice's statement to a fellow inmate did not violate the Confrontation Clause under the facts of that case, see *id.*, at 86-89, and I see no reason to foreclose the possibility that such statements, even those that inculpate a codefendant, may fall under a firmly rooted hearsay exception. The Court in *Dutton* recognized that statements to fellow prisoners, like confessions to family members or friends, bear sufficient indicia of reliability to be placed before a jury without confrontation of the declarant. *Id.*, at 89. Several federal courts have similarly concluded that such statements fall under a firmly rooted hearsay exception.[3] *Dutton* is thus no "exception," but a case wholly outside the "unbroken line" of cases, see *ante*, at 132, n.2, in which custodial confessions laying blame on a codefendant have been found to violate the Confrontation Clause. The custodial confession in this case falls under the coverage of this latter set of cases, and I would not extend the holding here any further.

The plurality's blanket ban on the government's use of accomplice statements that incriminate a defendant thus sweeps beyond the facts of this case and our precedent, ignoring both the exculpatory nature of Mark's confession and the circumstances in which it was given. Unlike the plurality, I would limit our holding here to the case at hand, and decide only that the Mark Lilly's custodial confession laying sole responsibility on petitioner cannot satisfy a firmly rooted hearsay exception.

---

[3]See, *e.g., United States v. York*, 933 F.2d 1343, 1362-1364 (CA7 1991) (finding federal declaration against penal interest exception firmly rooted in case involving accomplice's statements made to two associates); *United States v. Seeley*, 892 F.2d 1, 2 (CA1 1989) (exception firmly rooted in case involving statements made to declarant's girlfriend and stepfather); *United States v. Katsougrakis*, 715 F.2d 769, 776 (CA2 1983) (no violation in admitting accomplice's statements to friend).

II

Nor do I see any reason to do more than reverse the decision of the Supreme Court of Virginia and remand the case for the Commonwealth to demonstrate that Mark's confession bears "particularized guarantees of trustworthiness" under *Roberts*. The Supreme Court of Virginia held only that Mark Lilly's confession was admissible under a state law exception to its hearsay rules and then held that this exception was firmly rooted for Confrontation Clause purposes. See 499 S.E.2d 522, 533-534 (1998). Neither that court nor the trial court analyzed the confession under the second prong of the *Roberts* inquiry, and the discussion of reliability cited by the Court, pertained only to whether the confession should be admitted under state hearsay rules, not under the Confrontation Clause. Following our normal course, I see no reason for this Court to reach an issue upon which the lower courts did not pass. See *National Collegiate Athletic Assn. v. Smith*, 525 U.S. ----, ----, 119 S.Ct. 924, 930 (1999) ("[W]e do not decide in the first instance issues not decided below"). Thus, both this issue and the harmless-error question should be sent back to the Virginia courts.

The lack of any reviewable decision in this case makes especially troubling the plurality's conclusion that appellate courts must independently review a lower court's determination that a hearsay statement bears particularized guarantees of trustworthiness. Deciding whether a particular statement bears the proper indicia of reliability under our Confrontation Clause precedent "may be a mixed question of fact and law," but the mix weighs heavily on the "fact" side. We have said that "deferential review of mixed questions of law and fact is warranted when it appears that the district court is 'better positioned' than the appellate court to decide the issue in question or that probing appellate scrutiny will not contribute to the clarity of legal doctrine." *Salve Regina College v. Russell*, 499 U.S. 225, 233 (1991) (citation omitted).

These factors counsel in favor of deference to trial judges who undertake the second prong of the *Roberts* inquiry. They are better able to evaluate whether a particular statement given in a particular setting is sufficiently reliable that cross-examination would add little to its trustworthiness. Admittedly, this inquiry does not require credibility determinations, but we have already held that deference to district courts does not depend on the need for credibility determinations. See *Anderson v. Bessemer City*, 470 U.S. 564, 574 (1985).

Accordingly, I believe that in the setting here, as in *Anderson*, "[d]uplication of the trial judge's efforts in the court of appeals would very likely contribute only negligibly to the accuracy of fact determination at a huge cost in diversion of judicial resources." See *id.*, at 574-575. It is difficult to apply any standard in this case because none of the courts below conducted the second part of the *Roberts* inquiry. I would therefore remand this case to the Supreme Court of Virginia to carry out the inquiry, and, if any error is found, to determine whether that error is harmless.

[Insert at p. 520, after *Luce v. United States*]

## OHLER v. UNITED STATES

Supreme Court of the United States, 2000.
529 U.S. 753

REHNQUIST, C. J., delivered the opinion of the Court, in which O'CONNOR, SCALIA, KENNEDY, and THOMAS, JJ., joined. SOUTER, J., filed a dissenting opinion, in which STEVENS, GINSBURG, and BREYER, JJ., joined.

Petitioner, Maria Ohler, was arrested and charged with importation of marijuana and possession of marijuana with the intent to distribute. The District Court granted the Government's motion *in limine* seeking to admit evidence of her prior felony conviction as impeachment evidence under Federal Rule of Evidence 609(a)(1). Ohler testified at trial and admitted on direct examination that she had been convicted of possession of methamphetamine in 1993. The jury convicted her of both counts, and the Court of Appeals for the Ninth Circuit affirmed. We agree with the Court of Appeals that Ohler may not challenge the *in limine* ruling of the District Court on appeal.

Maria Ohler drove a van from Mexico to California in July 1997. As she passed through the San Ysidro Port of Entry, a customs inspector noticed that someone had tampered with one of the van's interior panels. Inspectors searched the van and discovered approximately 81 pounds of marijuana. Ohler was arrested and charged with importation of marijuana and possession of marijuana with the intent to distribute. Before trial, the Government filed motions *in limine* seeking to admit Ohler's prior felony conviction as character evidence under Federal Rule of Evidence 404(b) and as impeachment evidence under Rule 609(a)(1). The District Court denied the motion to admit the conviction as character evidence, but reserved ruling on whether the conviction could be used for impeachment purposes. On the first day of trial, the District Court ruled that if Ohler testified, evidence of her prior conviction would be admissible under Rule 609(a)(1). She testified in her own defense, denying any knowledge of the marijuana. She also admitted on direct examination that she had been convicted of possession of methamphetamine in 1993. The jury found Ohler guilty of both counts, and she was sentenced to 30 months in prison and 3 years' supervised release.

On appeal, Ohler challenged the District Court's *in limine* ruling allowing the Government to use her prior conviction for impeachment purposes. The Court of Appeals for the Ninth Circuit affirmed, holding that Ohler waived her objection by introducing evidence of the conviction during her direct examination. 169 F.3d 1200 (CA9 1999). We granted certiorari to resolve a conflict among the Circuits regarding whether appellate review of an *in limine* ruling is available in this situation. * * * We affirm.

Generally, a party introducing evidence cannot complain on appeal that the evidence was erroneously admitted. See 1 J. Weinstein & M. Berger, Weinstein's Federal Evidence § 103.14, 103-30 (2d ed. 2000). Cf. 1 J. Strong, McCormick on Evidence § 55, p. 246 (5th ed. 1999) ("If a party who has objected to evidence of a certain fact himself produces evidence from his own witness of the same fact, he has waived his objection."). Ohler seeks to avoid the consequences of this well-established common sense principle by invoking Rules 103 and 609 of the Federal Rules of Evidence. But neither of these Rules addresses the question at issue here. Rule 103 sets forth the unremarkable propositions that a party must make a timely objection to a ruling admitting evidence and that a party cannot challenge an evidentiary ruling unless it affects a substantial right.[1] The Rule does not purport to determine when a party waives a prior objection, and it is silent with respect to the effect of introducing evidence on direct examination, and later assigning its admission as error on appeal.

Rule 609(a) is equally unavailing for Ohler; it merely identifies the situations in which a witness' prior conviction may be admitted for impeachment purposes.[2] The Rule originally provided that admissible prior conviction evidence could be elicited from the defendant or established by public record during cross-examination, but it was amended in 1990 to clarify that the evidence could also be introduced on direct examination. According to Ohler, it follows from this amendment that a party does not waive her objection to the *in limine* ruling by introducing the evidence herself. However,

---

[1] Federal Rule of Evidence 103(a): "Error may not be predicated upon a ruling which admits or excludes evidence unless a substantial right of the party is affected, and (1) ... In case the ruling is one admitting evidence, a timely objection or motion to strike appears of record, stating the specific ground of objection, if the specific ground was not apparent from the context . . . ."

[2] Rule 609(a): "For the purpose of attacking the credibility of a witness, (1) evidence that a witness other than an accused has been convicted of a crime shall be admitted, subject to Rule 403, if the crime was punishable by death or imprisonment in excess of one year under the law under which the witness was convicted, and evidence that an accused has been convicted of such a crime shall be admitted if the court determines that the probative value of admitting this evidence out-weighs its prejudicial effect to the accused . . . ."

like Rule 103, Rule 609(a) simply does not address this issue. There is no question that the Rule authorizes the eliciting of a prior conviction on direct examination, but it does no more than that.

Next, Ohler argues that it would be unfair to apply such a waiver rule in this situation because it compels a defendant to forgo the tactical advantage of preemptively introducing the conviction in order to appeal the *in limine* ruling. She argues that if a defendant is forced to wait for evidence of the conviction to be introduced on cross-examination, the jury will believe that the defendant is less credible because she was trying to conceal the conviction. The Government disputes that the defendant is unduly disadvantaged by waiting for the prosecution to introduce the conviction on cross-examination. First, the Government argues that it is debatable whether jurors actually perceive a defendant to be more credible if she introduces a conviction herself. Second, even if jurors do consider the defendant more credible, the Government suggests that it is an unwarranted advantage because the jury does not realize that the defendant disclosed the conviction only after failing to persuade the court to exclude it.

Whatever the merits of these contentions, they tend to obscure the fact that both the Government and the defendant in a criminal trial must make choices as the trial progresses. For example, the defendant must decide whether or not to take the stand in her own behalf. If she has an innocent or mitigating explanation for evidence that might otherwise incriminate, acquittal may be more likely if she takes the stand. Here, for example, petitioner testified that she had no knowledge of the marijuana discovered in the van, that the van had been taken to Mexico without her permission, and that she had gone there simply to retrieve the van. But once the defendant testifies, she is subject to cross-examination, including impeachment by prior convictions, and the decision to take the stand may prove damaging instead of helpful. A defendant has a further choice to make if she decides to testify, notwithstanding a prior conviction. The defendant must choose whether to introduce the conviction on direct examination and remove the sting or to take her chances with the prosecutor's possible elicitation of the conviction on cross-examination.

The Government, too, in a case such as this, must make a choice. If the defendant testifies, it must choose whether or not to impeach her by use of her prior conviction. Here the trial judge had indicated he would allow its use,[2] but

---

[2]The District Court ruled on the first day of trial that Ohler's prior conviction would be admissible for impeachment purposes, and the court likely would have abided by that ruling at trial. However, *in limine* rulings are not binding on the trial judge, and the judge may always change his mind during the course of a trial. See *Luce v. United*

the Government still had to consider whether its use might be deemed reversible error on appeal. This choice is often based on the Government's appraisal of the apparent effect of the defendant's testimony. If she has offered a plausible, innocent explanation of the evidence against her, it will be inclined to use the prior conviction; if not, it may decide not to risk possible reversal on appeal from its use.

Due to the structure of trial, the Government has one inherent advantage in these competing trial strategies. Cross-examination comes after direct examination, and therefore the Government need not make its choice until the defendant has elected whether or not to take the stand in her own behalf and after the Government has heard the defendant testify.

Ohler's submission would deny to the Government its usual right to decide, after she testifies, whether or not to use her prior conviction against her. She seeks to short-circuit that decisional process by offering the conviction herself (and thereby removing the sting) and still preserve its admission as a claim of error on appeal.

But here Ohler runs into the position taken by the Court in a similar, but not identical, situation in *Luce v. United States*, 469 U.S. 38 (1984), that "[a]ny possible harm flowing from a district court's *in limine* ruling permitting impeachment by a prior conviction is wholly speculative." *Id.,* at 41. Only when the government exercises its option to elicit the testimony is an appellate court confronted with a case where, under the normal rules of trial, the defendant can claim the denial of a substantial right if in fact the district court's *in limine* ruling proved to be erroneous. In our view, there is nothing "unfair," as petitioner puts it, about putting petitioner to her choice in accordance with the normal rules of trial.

Finally, Ohler argues that applying this rule to her situation unconstitutionally burdens her right to testify. She relies on *Rock v. Arkansas*, 483 U.S. 44 (1987), where we held that a prohibition of hypnotically refreshed testimony interfered with the defendant's right to testify. But here the rule in question does not prevent Ohler from taking the stand and presenting any admissible testimony which she chooses. She is of course subject to cross-examination and subject to impeachment by the use of a prior conviction. In a sense, the use of these tactics by the Government may deter a defendant from

---

*States,* 469 U.S. 38, 41-42 (1984). Ohler's position, therefore, would deprive the trial court of the opportunity to change its mind after hearing all of the defendant's testimony.

taking the stand. But, as we said in *McGautha v. California,* 402 U.S. 183, 215 (1971):

> "It has long been held that a defendant who takes the stand in his own behalf cannot then claim the privilege against cross-examination on matters reasonably related to the subject matter of his direct examination . . . . It is not thought overly harsh in such situations to require that the determination whether to waive the privilege take into account the matters which may be brought out on cross-examination. It is also generally recognized that a defendant who takes the stand in his own behalf may be impeached by proof of prior convictions or the like . . . . Again, it is not thought inconsistent with the enlightened administration of criminal justice to require the defendant to weigh such pros and cons in deciding whether to testify."

For these reasons, we conclude that a defendant who preemptively introduces evidence of a prior conviction on direct examination may not on appeal claim that the admission of such evidence was error.

The judgment of the Court of Appeals for the Ninth Circuit is therefore affirmed.

*It is so ordered.*

Justice SOUTER, with whom Justice STEVENS, Justice GINSBURG, and Justice BREYER join, dissenting.

The majority holds that a testifying defendant perforce waives the right to appeal an adverse *in limine* ruling admitting prior convictions for impeachment. The holding is without support in precedent, the rules of evidence, or the reasonable objectives of trial, and I respectfully dissent.

The only case of this Court that the majority claims as even tangential support for its waiver rule is *Luce v. United States,* 469 U.S. 38 (1984). We held there that a criminal defendant who remained off the stand could not appeal an *in limine* ruling to admit prior convictions as impeachment evidence under Federal Rule of Evidence 609(a). Since the defendant had not testified, he had never suffered the impeachment, and the question was whether he should be allowed to appeal the *in limine* ruling anyway, on the rationale that the threatened impeachment had discouraged the exercise of his right to defend by his own testimony. The answer turned on the practical realities of appellate review.

An appellate court can neither determine why a defendant refused to testify, nor compare the actual trial with the one that would have occurred if the accused had taken the stand. With unavoidable uncertainty about whether and how much the *in limine* ruling harmed the defendant, and whether it affected the trial at all, a rule allowing a silent defendant to appeal would require courts either to attempt wholly speculative harmless-error analysis, or to grant new trials to some defendants who were not harmed by the ruling, and to some who never even intended to testify. In requiring testimony and actual impeachment before a defendant could appeal an *in limine* ruling to admit prior convictions, therefore, *Luce* did not derive a waiver rule from some general notion of fairness; it merely acknowledged the incapacity of an appellate court to assess the significance of the ruling for a defendant who remains silent.

This case is different, there being a factual record on which Ohler's claim can be reviewed. She testified, and there is no question that the *in limine* ruling controlled her counsel's decision to enquire about the earlier conviction; defense lawyers do not set out to impeach their own witnesses, much less their clients. Since analysis for harmless error is made no more difficult by the fact that the convictions came out on direct examination, not cross-examination, the case raises none of the practical difficulties on which *Luce* turned, and *Luce* does not dictate today's result.[1]

In fact, the majority's principal reliance is not on precedent but on the "common sense" rule that "a party introducing evidence cannot complain on appeal that the evidence was erroneously admitted." *Ante*, at 755. But this is no more support for today's holding than *Luce* is, for the common sense that approves the rule also limits its reach to a point well short of this case. The general rule makes sense, first, when a party who has freely chosen to introduce evidence of a particular fact later sees his opponent's evidence of the same fact erroneously admitted. He suffers no prejudice. See *Mercer v. Theriot,* 377 U.S. 152, 154 (1964) *(per curiam).* The rule makes sense, second, when the objecting party takes inconsistent positions, first requesting admission and then assigning error to the admission of precisely the same evidence at his opponent's behest. "The party should not be permitted 'to blow

---

[1] The *Luce* Court anticipated as much: "It is clear, of course, that had petitioner testified and been impeached by evidence of a prior conviction, the District Court's decision to admit the impeachment evidence would have been reviewable on appeal along with any other claims of error. The Court of Appeals would then have had a complete record detailing the nature of petitioner's testimony, the scope of the cross-examination, and the possible impact of impeachment on the jury's verdict." 469 U.S., at 41. There are, of course, practical issues that may arise in these cases; for example, the trial court may feel unable to render a final and definitive *in limine* ruling. The majority does not focus on these potential difficulties, and neither do I, though some lower courts have addressed them. See, *e.g., Wilson v. Williams,* 182 F.3d 562 (CA7 1999) (en banc). For the purpose of this case, we need consider only the circumstance in which a district court makes a ruling that is plainly final.

hot and cold' in this way." 1 J. Strong, McCormick on Evidence § 55, p. 246, n.14 (5th ed.1999).

Neither of these reasons applies when (as here) the defendant has opposed admission of the evidence and introduced it herself only to mitigate its effect in the hands of her adversary. Such a case falls beyond the scope of the general principle, and the scholarship almost uniformly treats it as exceptional. See, *e.g.,* 1 J. Wigmore, Evidence § 18, p. 836 (P. Tillers rev. 1983) ("[A] party who has made an unsuccessful motion in limine to exclude evidence that he expects the proponent to offer may be able to first to offer that same evidence without waiving his claim of error"); M. Graham, Handbook of Federal Evidence § 103.4, p. 17 (1981) ("However, the party may . . . himself bring out evidence ruled admissible over his objection to minimize its effect without it constituting a waiver of his objection"); 1 McCormick, *supra,* § 55, at 246 ("[W]hen [a party's] objection is made and overruled, he is entitled to treat this ruling as the 'law of the trial' and to explain or rebut, if he can, the evidence admitted over his protest"); D. Louisell & C. Mueller, Federal Evidence § 11, p. 65 (1977) ("Having done his best by objecting, the adversary would be indeed ill treated if then he was held to have thrown it all away by doing his best to protect his position by offering evidence of his own").[2] The general thrust of the law of evidence, then, not only fails to support the majority's approach, but points rather clearly in the other direction.

With neither precedent nor principle to support its chosen rule, the majority is reduced to saying that "there is nothing 'unfair' . . . about putting petitioner to her choice in accordance with the normal rules of trial."[3] *Ante,* at 759. Things are not this simple, however.

Any claim of a new rule's fairness under normal trial conditions will have to stand or fall on how well the rule would serve the objects that trials in general, and the Rules of Evidence in particular, are designed to achieve. Thus the provisions of Federal Rule of Evidence 102, that "[t]hese rules shall be

---

[2]The point on which the analysis of the cited treatises turns, it should be clear, is not which party first introduces the evidence, but rather which party seeks introduction and which exclusion. A defense lawyer who elicits testimony about prior convictions on direct examination, having failed in an attempt to have them excluded, is plainly making a defensive use of the convictions; he has no desire to impeach his client. The fact that it is the defense lawyer who first introduces the convictions, then, is irrelevant to the principle the majority invokes.

[3]For the reasons just given, this begs the question, which is whether the "normal rules of trial" apply beyond the normal circumstances for which they were devised.

construed to secure fairness in administration, elimination of unjustifiable expense and delay, and promotion of growth and development of the law of evidence to the end that the truth may be ascertained and proceedings justly determined." A judge's job, accordingly, is to curb the tactics of the trial battle in favor of weighing evidence calmly and getting to the most sensible understanding of whatever gave rise to the controversy before the court. The question is not which side gains a tactical advantage, but which rule assists in uncovering the truth. Today's new rule can make no such claim.

Previously convicted witnesses may testify honestly, but some convictions raise more than the ordinary question about the witness's readiness to speak truthfully. A factfinder who appreciates a heightened possibility of perjury will respond with heightened scrutiny, and when a defendant discloses prior convictions at the outset of her testimony, the jury will bear those convictions in mind as she testifies, and will scrutinize what she says more carefully. The purpose of Rule 609, in making some convictions admissible to impeach a witness's credibility, is thus fully served by a defendant's own testimony that the convictions occurred.

It is true that when convictions are revealed only on cross-examination, the revelation also warns the factfinder, but the timing of their disclosure may do more. The jury may feel that in testifying without saying anything about the convictions the defendant has meant to conceal them. The jury's assessment of the defendant's testimony may be affected not only by knowing that she has committed crimes in the past, but by blaming her for not being forthcoming when she seemingly could have been. Creating such an impression of current deceit by concealment is very much at odds with any purpose behind Rule 609, being obviously antithetical to dispassionate factfinding in support of a sound conclusion. The chance to create that impression is a tactical advantage for the Government, but only in the majority's dismissive sense of the term; it may affect the outcome of the trial, but only if it disserves the search for truth.

Allowing the defendant to introduce the convictions on direct examination thus tends to promote fairness of trial without depriving the Government of anything to which it is entitled. There is no reason to discourage the defendant from introducing the conviction herself, as the majority's waiver rule necessarily does.

# AMENDMENTS TO THE FEDERAL RULES OF EVIDENCE EFFECTIVE DECEMBER 1, 2000[*]

## Rule 103.  Rulings on Evidence

(a) Effect of erroneous ruling. — Error may not be predicated upon a ruling which admits or excludes evidence unless a substantial right of the party is affected, and

(1) Objection. — In case the ruling is one admitting evidence, a timely objection or motion to strike appears of record, stating the specific ground of objection, if the specific ground was not apparent from the context; or

(2) Offer of proof. — In case the ruling is one excluding evidence, the substance of the evidence was made known to the court by offer or was apparent from the context within which questions were asked.

<u>Once the court makes a definitive ruling on the record admitting or excluding evidence, either at or before trial, a party need not renew an objection or offer of proof to preserve a claim of error for appeal.</u>

(b) Record of offer and ruling. — The court may add any other or further statement which shows the character of the evidence, the form in which it was offered, the objection made, and the ruling thereon.  It may direct the making of an offer in question and answer form.

(c) Hearing of jury. — In jury cases, proceedings shall be conducted, to the extent practicable, so as to prevent inadmissible evidence from being suggested to the jury by any means, such as making statements or offers of proof or asking questions in the hearing of the jury.

(d) Plain error. — Nothing in this rule precludes taking notice of plain errors affecting substantial rights although they were not brought to the attention of the court.

---

[*]New matter is underlined; matter to be omitted is lined through.

## Rule 103

### Advisory Committee's Note (2000)

The amendment applies to all rulings on evidence whether they occur at or before trial, including so-called "*in limine*" rulings. One of the most difficult questions arising from *in limine* and other evidentiary rulings is whether a losing party must renew an objection or offer of proof when the evidence is or would be offered at trial, in order to preserve a claim of error on appeal. Courts have taken differing approaches to this question. Some courts have held that a renewal at the time the evidence is to be offered at trial is always required. *See, e.g., Collins v. Wayne Corp.*, 621 F.2d 777 (5th Cir. 1980). Some courts have taken a more flexible approach, holding that renewal is not required if the issue decided is one that (1) was fairly presented to the trial court for an initial ruling, (2) may be decided as a final matter before the evidence is actually offered, and (3) was ruled on definitively by the trial Judge. *See, e.g., Rosenffeld v. Basquiat*, 78 F.3d 84 (2d Cir. 1996) (admissibility of former testimony under the Dead Man's Statute; renewal not required). Other courts have distinguished between objections to evidence, which must be renewed when evidence is offered, and offers of proof, which need not be renewed after a definitive determination is made that the evidence is inadmissible. *See, e.g., Fusco v. General Motors Corp.*, 11 F.3d 259 (1st Cir. 1993). Another court, aware of this Committee's proposed amendment, has adopted its approach. *Wilson v. Williams*, 182 F.3d 562 (7th Cir. 1999) (en banc). Differing views on this question create uncertainty for litigants and unnecessary work for the appellate courts.

The amendment provides that a claim of error with respect to a definitive ruling is preserved for review when the party has otherwise satisfied the objection or offer of proof requirements of Rule 103(a). When the ruling is definitive, a renewed objection or offer of proof at the time the evidence is to be offered is more a formalism than a necessity. *See* Fed.R.Civ.P. 46 (formal exceptions unnecessary); Fed.R.Cr.P. 51 (same); *United States v. Mejia-Alarcon*, 995 F.2d 982, 986 (10th Cir. 1993) ("Requiring a party to renew an objection when the district court has issued a definitive ruling on a matter that can be fairly decided before trial would be in the nature of a formal exception and therefore unnecessary."). On the other hand, when the trial court appears to have reserved its ruling or to have indicated that the ruling is provisional, it makes sense to require the party to bring the issue to the court's attention subsequently. *See, e.g., United States v. Vest*, 116 F.3d 1179, 1188 (7th Cir. 1997) (where the trial court ruled *in limine* that testimony from defense witnesses could not be admitted, but allowed the defendant to seek leave at trial to call the witnesses should their testimony turn out to be relevant, the defendant's failure to seek such leave at trial meant that it was "too late to reopen the issue now on appeal"); *United States v. Valenti*, 60 F.3d 941 (2d Cir. 1995) (failure to proffer evidence at trial waives any claim of error where the trial judge had stated that he would reserve judgment on the *in limine* motion until he had heard the trial evidence).

The amendment imposes the obligation on counsel to clarify whether an *in limine* or other evidentiary ruling is definitive when there is doubt on that point. *See, e.g.,*

*Walden v. Georgia-Pacific Corp.*, 126 F.3d 506, 520 (3d Cir. 1997) (although "the district court told plaintiffs' counsel not to reargue every ruling, it did not countermand its clear opening statement that all of its rulings were tentative, and counsel never requested clarification, as he might have done.").

Even where the court's ruling is definitive, nothing in the amendment prohibits the court from revisiting its decision when the evidence is to be offered. If the court changes its initial ruling, or if the opposing party violates the terms of the initial ruling, objection must be made when the evidence is offered to preserve the claim of error for appeal. The error, if any, in such a situation occurs only when the evidence is offered and admitted. *United States Aviation Underwriters, Inc. v. Olympia Wings, Inc.*, 896 F.2d 949, 956 (5th Cir. 1990) ("objection is required to preserve error when an opponent, or the court itself, violates a motion *in limine* that was granted"); *United States v. Roenigk*, 810 F.2d 809 (8th Cir. 1987) (claim of error was not preserved where the defendant failed to object at trial to secure the benefit of a favorable advance ruling).

A definitive advance ruling is reviewed in light of the facts and circumstances before the trial court at the time of the ruling. If the relevant facts and circumstances change materially after the advance ruling has been made, those facts and circumstances cannot be relied upon on appeal unless they have been brought to the attention of the trial court by way of a renewed, and timely, objection, offer of proof, or motion to strike. *See Old Chief v. United States*, 519 U.S. 172, 182, n.6 (1997) ("it is important that a reviewing court evaluate the trial court's decision from its perspective when it had to rule and not indulge in review by hindsight."). Similarly, if the court decides in an advance ruling that proffered evidence is admissible subject to the eventual introduction by the proponent of a foundation for the evidence, and that foundation is never provided, the opponent cannot claim error based on the failure to establish the foundation unless the opponent calls that failure to the court's attention by a timely motion to strike or other suitable motion. *See Huddleston v. United States*, 485 U.S. 681, 690, n.7 (1988) ("It is, of course, not the responsibility of the judge *sua sponte* to ensure that the foundation evidence is offered; the objector must move to strike the evidence if at the close of the trial the offeror has failed to satisfy the condition.").

Nothing in the amendment is intended to affect the provisions of Fed.R.Civ.P. 72(a) or 28 U.S.C. § 636(b)(1) pertaining to nondispositive pretrial rulings by magistrate judges in proceedings that are not before a magistrate judge by consent of the parties. Fed. R. Civ. P. 72(a) provides that a party who fails to file a written objection to a magistrate judge's nondispositive order within ten days of receiving a copy "may not thereafter assign as error a defect" in the order. 28 U.S.C. § 636(b)(1) provides that any party "may serve and file written objections to such proposed findings and recommendations as provided by rules of court" within ten days of receiving a copy of the order. Several courts have held that a party must comply with this statutory provision in order to preserve a claim of error. *See, e.g., Wells v. Shriner's Hospital*, 109 F.3d 198, 200 (4th Cir. 1997) ("[i]n this circuit, as in others, a party 'may' file objections within ten days or he may not, as he chooses, but he 'shall' do so if he wishes further consideration."). When Fed.R.Civ.P. 72(a) or 28 U.S.C. § 636(b)(1) is operative, its requirement must be satisfied in order for a party to preserve a claim of error on appeal, even where Evidence Rule 103(a) would not require a subsequent objection or offer of proof.

Nothing in the amendment is intended to affect the rule set forth in *Luce v. United States*, 469 U.S. 38 (1984), and its progeny. The amendment provides that an objection or offer of proof need not be renewed to preserve a claim of error with respect to a definitive pretrial ruling. *Luce* answers affirmatively a separate question: whether a criminal defendant must testify at trial in order to preserve a claim of error predicated upon a trial court's decision to admit the defendant's prior convictions for impeachment. The *Luce* principle has been extended by many lower courts to other situations. *See United States v. DiMatteo*, 759 F.2d 831 (11th Cir. 1985) (applying *Luce* where the defendant's witness would be impeached with evidence offered under Rule 608). *See also United States v. Goldman*, 41 F.3d 785, 788 (1st Cir. 1994) ("Although *Luce* involved impeachment by conviction under Rule 609, the reasons given by the Supreme Court for requiring the defendant to testify apply with full force to the kind of Rule 403 and 404 objections that are advanced by *Goldman* in this case."); *Palmieri v. DeFaria*, 88 F.3d 136 (2d Cir. 1996) (where the plaintiff decided to take an adverse judgment rather than challenge an advance ruling by putting on evidence at trial, the *in limine* ruling would not be reviewed on appeal); *United States v. Ortiz*, 857 F.2d 900 (2d Cir. 1988) (where uncharged misconduct is ruled admissible if the defendant pursues a certain defense, the defendant must actually pursue that defense at trial in order to preserve a claim of error on appeal); *United States v. Bond*, 87 F.3d 695 (5th Cir. 1996) (where the trial court rules *in limine* that the defendant would waive his fifth amendment privilege were he to testify, the defendant must take the stand and testify in order to challenge that ruling on appeal).

The amendment does not purport to answer whether a party who objects to evidence that the court finds admissible in a definitive ruling, and who then offers the evidence to "remove the sting" of its anticipated prejudicial effect, thereby waives the right to appeal the trial court's ruling. *See, e.g., United States v. Fisher*, 106 F.3d 622 (5th Cir. 1997) (where the trial judge ruled *in limine* that the government could use a prior conviction to impeach the defendant if he testified, the defendant did not waive his right to appeal by introducing the conviction on direct examination); *Judd v. Rodman*, 105 F.3d 1339 (11th Cir. 1997) (an objection made *in limine* is sufficient to preserve a claim of error when the movant, as a matter of trial strategy, presents the objectionable evidence herself on direct examination to minimize its prejudicial effect); *Gill v. Thomas*, 83 F.3d 537, 540 (1st Cir. 1996) ("by offering the misdemeanor evidence himself, Gill waived his opportunity to object and thus did not preserve the issue for appeal"); *United States v. Williams*, 939 F.2d 721 (9th Cir. 1991) (objection to impeachment evidence was waived where the defendant was impeached on direct examination).

## Rule 404. Character Evidence Not Admissible to Prove Conduct; Exceptions; Other Crimes

(a) Character evidence generally. — Evidence of a person's character or a trait of character is not admissible for the purpose of proving action in conformity therewith on a particular occasion, except:

(1) Character of accused. — Evidence of a pertinent trait of character offered by an accused, or by the prosecution to rebut the same; or if evidence of a  trait of character of the alleged victim of the crime is offered by an accused and admitted under Rule 404 (a)(2), evidence of the same trait of character of the accused offered by the prosecution;

(2) Character of alleged victim. — Evidence of a pertinent trait of character of the alleged victim of the crime offered by an accused, or by the prosecution to rebut the same, or evidence of a character trait of peacefulness of the alleged victim offered by the prosecution in a homicide case to rebut evidence that the alleged victim was the first aggressor;

(3) Character of witness. — Evidence of the character of a witness, as provided in rules 607, 608, and 609.

(b) Other crimes, wrongs, or acts. — Evidence of other crimes, wrongs, or acts is not admissible to prove the character of a person in order to show action in conformity therewith.  It may, however, be admissible for other purposes, such as proof of motive, opportunity, intent, preparation, plan, knowledge, identity, or absence of mistake or accident, provided that upon request by the accused, the prosecution in a criminal case shall provide reasonable notice in advance of trial, or during trial if the court excuses pretrial notice on good cause shown, of the general nature of any such evidence it intends to introduce at trial.

### Rule 404(a)

#### Advisory Committee's Note (2000)

Rule 404(a)(1) has been amended to provide that when the accused attacks the character of an alleged victim under subdivision (a)(2) of this Rule, the door is opened to an attack on the same character trait of the accused.  Current law does not allow the government to introduce negative character evidence as to the accused unless the accused introduces evidence of good character. *See, e.g., United States v. Fountain,* 768 F.2d 790 (7th Cir. 1985) (when the accused offers proof of self-defense, this permits proof of the alleged victim's character trait for peacefulness, but it does not permit proof of the accused's character trait for violence).

The amendment makes clear that the accused cannot attack the alleged victim's character and yet remain shielded from the disclosure of equally relevant evidence concerning the same character trait of the accused. For example, in a murder case with a claim of self-defense, the accused, to bolster this defense, might offer evidence of the alleged victim's violent disposition. If the government has evidence that the accused has a violent character, but is not allowed to offer this evidence as part of its rebuttal, the jury has only part of the information it needs for an informed assessment of the probabilities as to who was the initial aggressor. This may be the case even if evidence of the accused's prior violent acts is admitted under Rule 404(b), because such evidence can be admitted only for limited purposes and not to show action in conformity with the accused's character on a specific occasion. Thus, the amendment is designed to permit a more balanced presentation of character evidence when an accused chooses to attack the character of the alleged victim.

The amendment does not affect the admissibility of evidence of specific acts of uncharged misconduct offered for a purpose other than proving character under Rule 404(b). Nor does it affect the standards for proof of character by evidence of other sexual behavior or sexual offenses under Rules 412-415. By its placement in Rule 404(a)(1), the amendment covers only proof of character by way of reputation or opinion.

The amendment does not permit proof of the accused's character if the accused merely uses character evidence for a purpose other than to prove the alleged victim's propensity to act in a certain way. *See United States v. Burks*, 470 F.2d 432, 434-5 (D.C. Cir. 1972) (evidence of the alleged victim's violent character, when known by the accused, was admissible "on the issue of whether or not the defendant reasonably feared he was in danger of imminent great bodily harm"). Finally, the amendment does not permit proof of the accused's character when the accused attacks the alleged victim's character as a witness under Rule 608 or 609.

The term "alleged" is inserted before each reference to "victim" in the Rule, in order to provide consistency with Evidence Rule 412.

## Rule 701. Opinion Testimony by Lay Witnesses

If the witness is not testifying as an expert, the witness' testimony in the form of opinions or inferences is limited to those opinions or inferences which are (a) rationally based on the perception of the witness, and (b) helpful to a clear understanding of the witness' testimony or the determination of a fact in issue, <u>and (c) not based on scientific technical, or other specialized knowledge within the scope of Rule 702.</u>

# Rule 701

## Advisory Committee's Note (2000)

Rule 701 has been amended to eliminate the risk that the reliability requirements set forth in Rule 702 will be evaded through the simple expedient of proffering an expert in lay witness clothing. Under the amendment, a witness' testimony must be scrutinized under the rules regulating expert opinion to the extent that the witness is providing testimony based on scientific, technical, or other specialized knowledge within the scope of Rule 702. *See generally Asplundh Mfg. Div. v. Benton Harbor Eng'g*, 57 F.3d 1190 (3d Cir. 1995). By channeling testimony that is actually expert testimony to Rule 702, the amendment also ensures that a party will not evade the expert witness disclosure requirements set forth in Fed.R.Civ.P. 26 and Fed.R.Crim.P. 16 by simply calling an expert witness in the guise of a layperson. *See* Joseph, *Emerging Expert Issues Under the 1993 Disclosure Amendments to the Federal Rules of Civil Procedure*, 164 F.R.D. 97, 108 (1996) (noting that "there is no good reason to allow what is essentially surprise expert testimony," and that "the Court should be vigilant to preclude manipulative conduct designed to thwart the expert disclosure and discovery process"). *See also United States v. Figueroa-Lopez*, 125 F.3d 1241, 1246 (9th Cir. 1997) (law enforcement agents testifying that the defendant's conduct was consistent with that of a drug trafficker could not testify as lay witnesses; to permit such testimony under Rule 701 "subverts the requirements of Federal Rule of Criminal Procedure 16(a)(1)(E)").

The amendment does not distinguish between expert and lay *witnesses*, but rather between expert and lay *testimony*. Certainly it is possible for the same witness to provide both lay and expert testimony in a single case. *See, e.g., United States v. Figueroa-Lopez*, 125 F.3d 1241, 1246 (9th Cir. 1997) (law enforcement agents could testify that the defendant was acting suspiciously, without being qualified as experts; however, the rules on experts were applicable where the agents testified on the basis of extensive experience that the defendant was using code words to refer to drug quantities and prices). The amendment makes clear that any part of a witness' testimony that is based upon scientific, technical, or other specialized knowledge within the scope of Rule 702 is governed by the standards of Rule 702 and the corresponding disclosure requirements of the Civil and Criminal Rules.

The amendment is not intended to affect the "prototypical example[s] of the type of evidence contemplated by the adoption of Rule 701 relat[ting] to the appearance of persons or things, identity, the manner of conduct, competency of a person, degrees of light or darkness, sound, size, weight, distance, and an endless number of items that cannot be described factually in words apart from inferences." *Asplundh Mfg. Div. v. Benton Harbor Eng'g*, 57 F.3d 1190, 1196 (3d Cir. 1995).

For example, most courts have permitted the owner or officer of a business to testify to the value or projected profits of the business, without the necessity of qualifying the witness as an accountant, appraiser, or similar expert. *See, e.g., Lightning Lube, Inc. v. Witco Corp.* 4 F.3d 1153 (3d Cir. 1993) (no abuse of discretion in permitting the plaintiff's owner to give lay opinion testimony as to damages, as it was based on his knowledge and participation in the day-to-day affairs of the business). Such opinion testimony is admitted not because of experience, training or specialized knowledge within the realm of an expert, but because of the particularized knowledge that the witness has by virtue of his or her position in the business. The amendment does not purport to change this analysis. Similarly, courts have permitted lay witnesses to testify that a substance appeared to be a narcotic, so long as a foundation of familiarity with the substance is established. *See, e.g., United States v. Westbrook*, 896 F.2d 330 (8th Cir. 1990) (two lay witnesses who were heavy amphetamine users were properly permitted to testify that a substance was amphetamine; but it was error to permit another witness to make such an identification where she had no experience with amphetamines). Such testimony is not based on specialized knowledge within the scope of Rule 702, but rather is based upon a layperson's personal knowledge. If, however, that witness were to describe how a narcotic was manufactured, or to describe the intricate workings of a narcotic distribution network, then the witness would have to qualify as an expert under Rule 702. *United States v. Figueroa-Lopez, supra.*

The amendment incorporates the distinctions set forth in *State v. Brown*, 836 S.W.2d 530, 549 (1992), a case involving former Tennessee Rule of Evidence 701, a rule that precluded lay witness testimony based on "special knowledge." In *Brown*, the court declared that the distinction between lay and expert witness testimony is that lay testimony "results from a process of reasoning familiar in everyday life," while expert testimony "results from a process of reasoning which can be mastered only by specialists in the field." The court in *Brown* noted that a lay witness with experience could testify that a substance appeared to be blood, but that a witness would have to qualify as an expert before he could testify that bruising around the eyes is indicative of skull trauma. That is the kind of distinction made by the amendment to this Rule.

## Rule 702. Testimony by Experts

If scientific, technical, or other specialized knowledge will assist the trier of fact to understand the evidence or to determine a fact in issue, a witness qualified as an expert by knowledge, skill, experience, training, or education, may testify thereto in the form of an opinion or otherwise, <u>if (1) the testimony is based on sufficient facts or data, (2) the testimony is the product of reliable principles and methods, and (3) the witness has applied the principles and methods reliably to the facts of the case.</u>

### Rule 702

#### Advisory Committee's Note (2000)

Rule 702 has been amended in response to *Daubert v. Merrell Dow Pharmaceuticals, Inc.*, 509 U.S. 579 (1993), and to the many cases applying *Daubert*, including *Kumho Tire Co. v. Carmichael*, 119 S.Ct. 1167 (1999). In *Daubert* the Court charged trial judges with the responsibility of acting as gatekeepers to exclude unreliable expert testimony, and the Court in *Kumho* clarified that this gatekeeper function applies to all expert testimony, not just testimony based in science. See also *Kumho*, 119 S.Ct. at 1178 (citing the Committee Note to the proposed amendment to Rule 702, which had been released for public comment before the date of the *Kumho* decision). The amendment affirms the trial court's role as gatekeeper and provides some general standards that the trial court must use to assess the reliability and helpfulness of proffered expert testimony. Consistently with *Kumho*, the Rule as amended provides that all types of expert testimony present questions of admissibility for the trial court in deciding whether the evidence is reliable and helpful. Consequently, the admissibility of all expert testimony is governed by the principles of Rule 104(a). Under that Rule, the proponent has the burden of establishing that the pertinent admissibility requirements are met by a preponderance of the evidence. *See Bourjaily v. United States*, 483 U.S. 171 (1987).

*Daubert* set forth a non-exclusive checklist for trial courts to use in assessing the reliability of scientific expert testimony. The specific factors explicated by the *Daubert* Court are (1) whether the expert's technique or theory can be or has been tested that is, whether the expert's theory can be challenged in some objective sense, or whether it is instead simply a subjective, conclusory approach that cannot reasonably be assessed for reliability; (2) whether the technique or theory has been subject to peer review and publication; (3) the known or potential rate of error of the technique or theory when applied; (4) the existence and maintenance of standards and controls; and (5) whether the technique or theory has been generally accepted in the scientific community. The Court in *Kumho* held that these factors might also be applicable in assessing the reliability of non-scientific expert testimony, depending upon "the particular circumstances of the particular case at issue." 119 S.Ct. at 1175.

No attempt has been made to "codify" these specific factors. *Daubert* itself emphasized that the factors were neither exclusive nor dispositive. Other cases have recognized that not all of the specific *Daubert* factors can apply to every type of expert testimony. In addition to *Kumho*, 119 S.Ct. at 1175, *see Tyus v. Urban Search Management*, 102 F.3d 256 (7th Cir. 1996) (noting that the factors mentioned by the Court in *Daubert* do not neatly apply to expert testimony from a sociologist). *See also Kannankeril v. Terminix Int'l, Inc.*, 128 F.3d 802, 809 (3d Cir. 1997) (holding that lack of peer review or publication was not dispositive where the expert's opinion was supported by "widely accepted scientific knowledge"). The standards set forth in the amendment are broad enough to require consideration of any or all of the specific *Daubert* factors where appropriate.

Courts both before and after *Daubert* have found other factors relevant in determining whether expert testimony is sufficiently reliable to be considered by the trier of fact. These factors include:

(1) Whether experts are "proposing to testify about matters growing naturally and directly out of research they have conducted independent of the litigation, or whether they have developed their opinions expressly for purposes of testifying." *Daubert v. Merrell Dow Pharmaceuticals, Inc.*, 43 F.3d 1311, 1317 (9th Cir. 1995).

(2) Whether the expert has unjustifiably extrapolated from an accepted premise to an unfounded conclusion. *See General Elec. Co. v. Joiner*, 522 U.S. 136, 146

(1997) (noting that in some cases a trial court "may conclude that there is simply too great an analytical gap between the data and the opinion proffered").

(3) Whether the expert has adequately accounted for obvious alternative explanations. *See Claar v. Burlington N.R.R.*, 29 F.3d 499 (9th Cir. 1994) (testimony excluded where the expert failed to consider other obvious causes for the plaintiff's condition). *Compare Ambrosini v. Labarraque*, 101 F.3d 129 (D.C. Cir. 1996) (the possibility of some uneliminated causes presents a question of weight, so long as the most obvious causes have been considered and reasonably ruled out by the expert).

(4) Whether the expert "is being as careful as he would be in his regular professional work outside his paid litigation consulting." *Sheehan v. Daily Racing Form, Inc.*, 104 F.3d 940, 942 (7th Cir. 1997). *See Kumho Tire Co. v. Carmichael*, 119 S.Ct. 1167, 1176 (1999) (*Daubert* requires the trial court to assure itself that the expert "employs in the courtroom the same level of intellectual rigor that characterizes the practice of an expert in the relevant field.").

(5) Whether the field of expertise claimed by the expert is known to reach reliable results for the type of opinion the expert would give. *See Kumho Tire Co. v. Carmichael*, 119 S.Ct. 1167, 1175 (1999) (*Daubert's* general acceptance factor does not "help show that an expert's testimony is reliable where the discipline itself lacks reliability, as, for example, do theories grounded in any so-called generally accepted principles of astrology or *Moore v. Ashland Chemical, Inc.*, 151 F.3d 269 necromancy."); (5th Cir. 1998) (en banc) (clinical doctor was properly precluded from testifying to the toxicological cause of the plaintiff's respiratory problem, where the opinion was not sufficiently grounded in scientific methodology); *Sterling v. Velsicol Chem. Corp.*, 855 F.2d 1188 (6th Cir. 1988) (rejecting testimony based on "clinical ecology" as unfounded and unreliable).

All of these factors remain relevant to the determination of the reliability of expert testimony under the Rule as amended. Other factors may also be relevant. See *Kumho*, 119 S.Ct. 1167, 1176 ("[W]e conclude that the trial judge must have considerable leeway in deciding in a particular case how to go about determining whether particular expert testimony is reliable."). Yet no single factor is necessarily dispositive of the reliability of a particular expert's testimony. *See, e.g., Heller v. Shaw Industries, Inc.*, 167 F.3d 146, 155 (3d Cir. 1999) ("not only must each stage of the expert's testimony be reliable, but each stage must be evaluated practically and flexibly without bright-line exclusionary (or inclusionary) rules."); *Daubert v. Merrell Dow Pharmaceuticals, Inc.*, 43 F.3d 1311, 1317, n.5 (9th Cir. 1995) (noting that some expert disciplines "have the courtroom as a principal theatre of operations" and as to these disciplines "the fact that the expert has developed an expertise principally for purposes of litigation will obviously not be a substantial consideration.").

A review of the caselaw after *Daubert* shows that the rejection of expert testimony is the exception rather than the rule. *Daubert* did not work a "seachange over federal evidence law," and "the trial court's role as gatekeeper is not intended to serve as a replacement for the adversary system." *United States v. 14.38 Acres of Land Situated in Leflore County, Mississippi*, 80 F.3d 1074, 1078 (5th Cir. 1996). As the Court in

*Daubert* stated: "Vigorous cross-examination, presentation of contrary evidence, and careful instruction on the burden of proof are the traditional and appropriate means of attacking shaky but admissible evidence." 509 U.S. at 595. Likewise, this amendment is not intended to provide an excuse for an automatic challenge to the testimony of every expert. *See Kumho Tire Co. v. Carmichael*, 119 S.Ct. 1167, 1176 (1999) (noting that the trial judge has the discretion "both to avoid unnecessary 'reliability' proceedings in ordinary cases where the reliability of an expert's methods is property taken for granted, and to require appropriate proceedings in the less usual or more complex cases where cause for questioning the expert's reliability arises.").

When a trial court, applying this amendment, rules that an expert's testimony is reliable, this does not necessarily mean that contradictory expert testimony is unreliable. The amendment is broad enough to permit testimony that is the product of competing principles or methods in the same field of expertise. *See, e.g., Heller v. Shaw Industries, Inc.*, 167 F.3d 146, 160 (3d Cir. 1999) (expert testimony cannot be excluded simply because the expert uses one test rather than another, when both tests are accepted in the field and both reach reliable results). As the court stated in *In re Paoli R. R. Yard PCB Litigation*, 35 F.3d 717, 744 (3d Cir. 1994), proponents "do not have to demonstrate to the judge by a preponderance of the evidence that the assessments of their experts are correct, they only have to demonstrate by a preponderance of evidence that their opinions are reliable . . . . The evidentiary requirement of reliability is lower than the merits standard of correctness." *See also Daubert v. Merrell Dow Pharmaceuticals, Inc.*, 43 F.3d 1311, 1318 (9th Cir. 1995) (scientific experts might be permitted to testify if they could show that the methods they used were also employed by "a recognized minority of scientists in their field."); *Ruiz-Troche v. Pepsi Cola*, 161 F.3d 77, 85 (1st Cir. 1998) ("*Daubert* neither requires nor empowers trial courts to determine which of several competing scientific theories has the best provenance.").

The Court in *Daubert* declared that the "focus, of course, must be solely on principles and methodology, not on the conclusions they generate." 509 U.S. at 595. Yet as the Court later recognized, "conclusions and methodology are not entirely distinct from one another." *General Elec. Co. v. Joiner*, 522 U.S. 136, 146 (1997). Under the amendment, as under *Daubert*, when an expert purports to apply principles and methods in accordance with professional standards, and yet reaches a conclusion that other experts in the field would not reach, the trial court may fairly suspect that the principles and methods have not been faithfully applied. *See Lust v. Merrell Dow Pharmaceuticals, Inc.*, 89 F.3d 594, 598 (9th Cir. 1996). The amendment specifically provides that the trial court must scrutinize not only the principles and methods used by the expert, but also whether those principles and methods have been properly applied to the facts of the case. As the court noted in *In re Paoli R.R. Yard PCB Litig.*, 35 F.3d 717, 745 (3d Cir. 1994), "*any* step that renders the analysis unreliable . . . renders the expert's testimony inadmissible. *This is true whether the step completely changes a reliable methodology or merely misapplies that methodology.*"

If the expert purports to apply principles and methods to the facts of the case, it is important that this application be conducted reliably. Yet it might also be important in some cases for an expert to educate the factfinder about general principles, without ever attempting to apply these principles to the specific facts of the case. For example, experts might instruct the factfinder on the principles of thermodynamics, or bloodclotting, or on how financial markets respond to corporate reports, without ever knowing about or trying to tie their testimony into the facts of the case. The amendment does not alter the venerable practice of using expert testimony to educate the factfinder on general principles. For this kind of generalized testimony, Rule 702 simply requires that: (1) the expert be qualified; (2) the testimony address a subject matter on which the factfinder can be assisted by an expert; (3) the testimony be reliable; and (4) the testimony "fit" the facts of the case.

As stated earlier, the amendment does not distinguish between scientific and other forms of expert testimony. The trial court's gatekeeping function applies to testimony by any expert. *See Kumho Tire Co. v. Carmichael*, 119 S.Ct. 1167, 1171 (1999) ("We conclude that *Daubert's* general holding—setting forth the trial judge's general 'gatekeeping' obligation—applies not only to testimony based on 'scientific' knowledge, but also to testimony based on 'technical' and 'other specialized' knowledge."). While the relevant factors for determining reliability will vary from expertise to expertise, the amendment rejects the premise that an expert's testimony should be treated more permissively simply because it is outside the realm of science. An opinion from an expert who is not a scientist should receive the same degree of scrutiny for reliability as an opinion from an expert who purports to be a scientist. *See Watkins v. Telsmith, Inc.*. 121 F.3d 984, 991 (5th Cir. 1997) ("[I]t seems exactly backwards that experts who purport to rely on general engineering principles and practical experience might escape screening by the district court simply by stating that their conclusions were not reached by any particular method or technique."). Some types of expert testimony will be more objectively verifiable, and subject to the expectations of falsifiability, peer review, and publication, than others. Some types of expert testimony will not rely on anything like a scientific method, and so will have to be evaluated by reference to other standard principles attendant to the particular area of expertise. The trial judge in all cases of proffered expert testimony must find that it is properly grounded, well-reasoned, and not speculative before it can be admitted. The expert's testimony must be grounded in an accepted body of learning or experience in the expert's field, and the expert must explain how the conclusion is so grounded. *See, e.g.*, American College of Trial Lawyers, *Standards and Procedures for Determining the Admissibility of Expert Testimony after Daubert*, 157 F.R.D. 571, 579 (1994) ("[W]hether the testimony concerns economic principles, accounting standards, property valuation or other non-scientific subjects, it should be evaluated by reference to the 'knowledge and experience' of that particular field.").

The amendment requires that the testimony must be the product of reliable principles and methods that are reliably applied to the facts of the case. While the terms "principles" and "methods" may convey a certain impression when applied to scientific knowledge, they remain relevant when applied to testimony based on technical or other specialized knowledge. For example, when a law enforcement agent testifies regarding the use of code words in a drug transaction, the principle used by the agent is that participants in such transactions regularly use code words to conceal the nature of their activities. The method used by the agent is the application of extensive experience to analyze the meaning of the conversations. So long as the principles and methods are reliable and applied reliably to the facts of the case, this type of testimony should be admitted.

Nothing in this amendment is intended to suggest that experience alone — or experience in conjunction with other knowledge, skill, training or education — may not provide a sufficient foundation for expert testimony. To the contrary, the text of Rule 702 expressly contemplates that an expert may be qualified on the basis of experience. In certain fields, experience is the predominant, if not sole, basis for a great deal of reliable expert testimony. *See, e.g., United States v. Jones*, 107 F.3d 1147 (6th Cir. 1997) (no abuse of discretion in admitting the testimony of a handwriting examiner who had years of practical experience and extensive training, and who explained his methodology in detail); *Tassin v. Sears Roebuck*, 946 F.Supp. 1241, 1248 (M.D. La. 1996) (design engineer's testimony can be admissible when the expert's opinions "are based on facts, a reasonable investigation, and traditional technical/mechanical expertise, and he provides a reasonable link between the information and procedures he uses and the conclusions he reaches"). *See also Kumho Tire Co. v. Carmichael*, 119 S.Ct. 1167, 1178 (1999) (stating that "no one denies that an expert might draw a conclusion from a set of observations based on extensive and specialized experience.").

If the witness is relying solely or primarily on experience, then the witness must explain how that experience leads to the conclusion reached, why that experience is a sufficient basis for the opinion, and how that experience is reliably applied to the facts. The trial court's gatekeeping function requires more than simply "taking the expert's word for it." *See Daubert v. Merrell Dow Pharmaceuticals, Inc.*, 43 F.3d 1311, 1319 (9th Cir. 1995) ("We've been presented with only the experts' qualifications, their conclusions and their assurances of reliability. Under *Daubert*, that's not enough."). The more subjective and controversial the expert's inquiry, the more likely the testimony should be excluded as unreliable. *See O'Conner v. Commonwealth Edison Co.*, 13 F.3d 1090 (7th Cir. 1994) (expert testimony based on a completely subjective methodology held property excluded). *See also Kumho Tire Co. v. Carmichael*, 119 S.Ct. 1167, 1176 (1999) ("[I]t will at times be useful to ask even of a witness whose expertise is based purely on experience, say, a perfume tester able to distinguish among 140 odors at a sniff, whether his preparation is of a kind that others in the field would recognize as acceptable.").

Subpart (1) of Rule 702 calls for a quantitative rather than qualitative analysis. The amendment requires that expert testimony be based on sufficient underlying "facts or data." The term "data" is intended to encompass the reliable opinions of other experts. See the original Advisory Committee Note to Rule 703. The language "facts or data" is broad enough to allow an expert to rely on hypothetical facts that are supported by the evidence. *Id.*

When facts are in dispute, experts sometimes reach different conclusions based on competing versions of the facts. The emphasis in the amendment on "sufficient facts or data" is not intended to authorize a trial court to exclude an expert's testimony on the ground that the court believes one version of the facts and not the other.

There has been some confusion over the relationship between Rules 702 and 703. The amendment makes clear that the sufficiency of the basis of an expert's testimony is to be decided under Rule 702. Rule 702 sets forth the overarching requirement of reliability, and an analysis of the sufficiency of the expert's basis cannot be divorced from the ultimate reliability of the expert's opinion. In contrast, the "reasonable reliance" requirement of Rule 703 is a relatively narrow inquiry. When an expert relies on inadmissible information, Rule 703 requires the trial court to determine whether that information is of a type reasonably relied on by other experts in the field. If so, the expert can rely on the information in reaching an opinion. However, the question whether the expert is relying on a *sufficient* basis of information—whether admissible information or not—is governed by the requirements of Rule 702.

The amendment makes no attempt to set forth procedural requirements for exercising the trial court's gatekeeping function over expert testimony. *See* Daniel J. Capra, *The Daubert Puzzle*, 38 Ga. L. Rev. 699, 766 (1998) ("Trial courts should be allowed substantial discretion in dealing with *Daubert* questions; any attempt to codify procedures will likely give rise to unnecessary changes in practice and create difficult questions for appellate review."). Courts have shown considerable ingenuity and flexibility in considering challenges to expert testimony under *Daubert*, and it is contemplated that this will continue under the amended Rule. *See, e.g., Cortes-Irizarry v. Corporacion Insular*, 111 F.3d 184 (1st Cir. 1997) (discussing the application of *Daubert* in ruling on a motion for summary judgment); *In re Paoli R.R. Yard PCB Litig.*, 35 F.3d 717, 736, 739 (3d Cir. 1994) (discussing the use of *in limine* hearings); *Claar v. Burlington N.R.R.*, 29 F.3d 499, 502-05 (9th Cir. 1994) (discussing the trial court's technique of ordering experts to submit serial affidavits explaining the reasoning and methods underlying their conclusions).

The amendment continues the practice of the original Rule in referring to a qualified witness as an "expert." This was done to provide continuity and to minimize change. The use of the term "expert" in the Rule does not, however, mean that a jury should actually be informed that a qualified witness is testifying as an "expert." Indeed, there is much to be said for a practice that prohibits the use of the term "expert" by both the parties and the court at trial. Such a practice "ensures that trial courts do not inadvertently put their stamp of authority" on a witness's opinion, and protects against the jury's being "overwhelmed by the so-called 'experts'." Hon. Charles Richey, *Proposals To Eliminate the Prejudicial Effect of the Use of the Word "Expert" Under the Federal Rules of Evidence in Criminal and Civil Jury Trials*, 154 F.R.D. 537, 559 (1994) (setting forth limiting instructions and a standing order employed to prohibit the use of the term "expert" in jury trials).

## Rule 703. Bases of Opinion Testimony by Experts

The facts or data in the particular case upon which an expert bases an opinion or inference may be those perceived by or made known to the expert at or before the hearing. If of a type reasonably relied upon by experts in the particular field in forming opinions or inferences upon the subject, the facts or data need not be admissible in evidence <u>in order for the opinion or inference to be admitted.  Facts or data that are otherwise inadmissible shall not be disclosed to the jury by the proponent of the opinion or inference unless the court determines that their probative value in assisting the jury to evaluate the expert's opinion substantially outweighs their prejudicial effect.</u>

**Rule 703**

**Advisory Committee's Note (2000)**

Rule 703 has been amended to emphasize that when an expert reasonably relies on inadmissible information to form an opinion or inference, the underlying information is not admissible simply because the opinion or inference is admitted.  Courts have reached different results on how to treat inadmissible information when it is reasonably relied upon by an expert in forming an opinion or drawing an inference.  *Compare United States v. Rollins*, 862 F.2d 1282 (7th Cir. 1988) (admitting, as part of the basis of an FBI agent's expert opinion on the meaning of code language, the hearsay statements of an informant), with *United States v. 0.59 Acres of Land*, 109 F.3d 1493 (9th Cir. 1997) (error to admit hearsay offered as the basis of an expert opinion, without a limiting instruction).  Commentators have also taken differing views. *See, e.g.*, Ronald Carlson, *Policing the Bases of Modern Expert Testimony*, 39 Vand. L. Rev. 577 (1986) (advocating limits on the jury's consideration of otherwise inadmissible evidence used as the basis for an expert opinion); Paul Rice, *Inadmissible Evidence as a Basis for Expert Testimony: A Response to Professor Carlson*, 40 Vand. L. Rev. 583 (1987) (advocating unrestricted use of information reasonably relied upon by an expert).

When information is reasonably relied upon by an expert and yet is admissible only for the purpose of assisting the jury in evaluating an expert's opinion, a trial court applying this Rule must consider the information's probative value in assisting the jury to weigh the expert's opinion on the one hand, and the risk of prejudice resulting from the jury's potential misuse of the information for substantive purposes on the other. The information may be disclosed to the jury, upon objection, only if the trial court finds that the probative value of the information in assisting the jury to evaluate the expert's opinion substantially outweighs its prejudicial effect.  If the otherwise inadmissible information is admitted under this balancing test, the trial judge must give a limiting instruction upon request, informing the jury that the underlying information must not be used for substantive purposes. *See* Rule 105.  In determining the appropriate course, the trial court should consider the probable effectiveness or lack of effectiveness of a limiting instruction under the particular circumstances.

The amendment governs only the disclosure to the jury of information that is reasonably relied on by an expert, when that information is not admissible for substantive purposes.  It is not intended to affect the admissibility of an expert's testimony. Nor does the amendment prevent an expert from relying on information that is inadmissible for substantive purposes.

Nothing in this Rule restricts the presentation of underlying expert facts or data when offered by an adverse party. *See* Rule 705. Of course, an adversary's attack on an expert's basis will often open the door to a proponent's rebuttal with information that was reasonably relied upon by the expert even if that information would not have been discloseable initially under the balancing test provided by this amendment. Moreover, in some circumstances the proponent might wish to disclose information that is relied upon by the expert in order to "remove the sting" from the opponent's anticipated attack, and thereby prevent the jury from drawing an unfair negative inference. The trial court should take this consideration into account in applying the balancing test provided by this amendment.

This amendment covers facts or data that cannot be admitted for any purpose other than to assist the jury to evaluate the expert's opinion. The balancing test provided in this amendment is not applicable to facts or data that are admissible for any other purpose but have not yet been offered for such a purpose at the time the expert testifies.

The amendment provides a presumption against disclosure to the jury of information used as the basis of an expert's opinion and not admissible for any substantive purpose, when that information is offered by the proponent of the expert. In a multi-party case, where one party proffers an expert whose testimony is also beneficial to other parties, each such party should be deemed a "proponent" within the meaning of the amendment.

## Rule 803. Hearsay. Exceptions; Availability of Declarant Immaterial

The following are not excluded by the hearsay rule, even though the declarant is available as a witness:

\* \* \*

(6) Records of regularly conducted activity. — A memorandum, report, record, or data compilation, in any form, of acts, events, conditions, opinions, or diagnoses, made at or near the time by, or from information transmitted by, a person with knowledge, if kept in the course of a regularly conducted business activity, and if it was the regular practice of that business activity to make the memorandum, report record or data compilation, all as shown by the testimony of the custodian or other qualified witness, <u>or by certification that complies with Rule 902(11), Rule 902(12) or a statute permitting certification,</u> unless the source of information or the method or circumstances of preparation indicate lack of trustworthiness. The term "business" as used in this paragraph includes business, institution, association, profession,

occupation, and calling of every kind, whether or not conducted for profit.

*   *   *

### Rule 803(6)

#### Advisory Committee's Note (2000)

The amendment provides that the foundation requirements of Rule 803(6) can be satisfied under certain circumstances without the expense and inconvenience of producing time-consuming foundation witnesses. Under current law, courts have generally required foundation witnesses to testify. *See, e.g., Tongil Co., Ltd v. Hyundai Merchant Marine Corp.*, 968 F.2d 999 (9th Cir. 1992) (reversing a judgment based on business records where a qualified person filed an affidavit but did not testify). Protections are provided by the authentication requirements of Rule 902(11) for domestic records, Rule 902(12) for foreign records in civil cases, and 18 U.S.C. § 3505 for foreign records in criminal cases.

## Rule 902. Self-authentication

Extrinsic evidence of authenticity as a condition precedent to admissibility is not required with respect to the following:

*   *   *

(11) Certified domestic records of regularly conducted activity. — The original or a duplicate of a domestic record of regularly conducted activity that would be admissible under Rule 803(6) if accompanied by a written declaration of its custodian or other qualified person, in a manner complying with any Act of Congress or rule prescribed by the Supreme Court pursuant to statutory authority, certifying that the record

(A) was made at or near the time of the occurrence of the matters set forth by, or from information transmitted by, a person with knowledge of these matters;

(B) was kept in the course of the regularly conducted activity; and

(C) was made by the regularly conducted activity as a regular practice.

A party intending to offer a record of evidence under this paragraph must provide written notice of that intention to all adverse parties, and must make the record and declaration available for inspection

48

sufficiently in advance of their offer into evidence to provide an adverse party with a fair opportunity to challenge them.

(12) Certified foreign records of regularly conducted activity. In a civil case, the original or a duplicate of a foreign record activity that would be admissible under Rule 803(6) if accompanied by a written declaration by its custodian or other qualified person certifying that the record—

(A) was made at or near the time of the occurrence of the matters set forth by, or from information transmitted by, a person with knowledge of those matters;

(B) was kept in the course of the regularly conducted activity; and

(C) was made by the regularly conducted activity as a regular practice.

The declaration must be signed in a manner that, if falsely made, would subject the maker to criminal penalty under the laws of the country where the declaration is signed. A party intending to offer a record into evidence under this paragraph must provide written notice of that intention to all adverse parties, and must make the record and declaration available for inspection sufficiently in advance of their offer to provide an adverse party with a fair opportunity to challenge them.

## Rule 902
### Advisory Committee's Note (2000)

The amendment adds two new paragraphs to the rule on self-authentication. It sets forth a procedure by which parties can authenticate certain records of regularly conducted activity, other than through the testimony of a foundation witness. See the amendment to Rule 803(6). 18 U.S.C. § 3505 currently provides a means for certifying foreign records of regularly conducted activity in criminal cases, and this amendment is intended to establish a similar procedure for domestic records, and for foreign records offered in civil cases.

A declaration that satisfies 28 U.S.C. § 1746 would satisfy the declaration requirement of Rule 902(11), as would any comparable certification under oath.

The notice requirement in Rules 902(11) and (12) is intended to give the opponent of the evidence a full opportunity to test the adequacy of the foundation set forth in the declaration.

# PROPOSED AMENDMENTS TO THE FEDERAL RULES OF EVIDENCE

## Proposed Rule 608.  Evidence of Character and Conduct of Witness (June 2002)[*]

(a) Opinion and reputation evidence of character. — The credibility of a witness may be attacked or supported by evidence in the form of opinion or reputation, but subject to these limitations:

(1) the evidence may refer only to character for truthfulness or untruthfulness, and

(2) evidence of truthful character is admissible only after the character of the witness for truthfulness has been attacked by opinion or reputation evidence or otherwise.

(b) Specific instances of conduct. — Specific instances of the conduct of a witness, for the purpose of attacking or supporting the witness' ~~credibility~~ character for truthfulness, other than conviction of crime as provided in Rule 609, may not be proved by extrinsic evidence.  They may, however, in the discretion of the court, if probative of truthfulness or untruthfulness, be inquired into on cross- examination of the witness (1) concerning the witness' character for truthfulness or untruthfulness, or (2) concerning the character for truthfulness or untruthfulness of another witness as to which character the witness being cross-examined has testified.

The giving of testimony, whether by an accused or by any other witness, does not operate as a waiver of the accused's or the witness' privilege against self-incrimination when examined with respect to matters ~~which~~ that relate only to ~~credibility~~ character for truthfulness.

---

[*]New matter is underlined and matter to be omitted is lined through.  [As this Supplement went to press, the amendment to Rule 608(b) had been approved by the Standing Committee and transmitted to the Judicial Conference.  If all goes smoothly, it will be promulgated by the Supreme Court and become effective on December 1, 2003  -Eds.]

## Proposed Rule 608
### Advisory Committee Notes (2002)

The Rule has been amended to clarify that the absolute prohibition on extrinsic evidence applies only when the sole reason for proffering that evidence is to attack or support the witness' character for truthfulness. *See United States v. Abel*, 469 U.S. 45 (1984); *United States v. Fusco*, 748 F.2d 996 (5th Cir. 1984) (Rule 608(b) limits the use of evidence "designed to show that the witness has done things, unrelated to the suit being tried, that make him more or less believable per se"); Ohio R. Evid. 608(b). On occasion the Rule's use of the overbroad term "credibility" has been read "to bar extrinsic evidence for bias, competency and contradiction impeachment since they too deal with credibility." American Bar Association Section of Litigation, *Emerging Problems Under the Federal Rules of Evidence* at 161 (3d ed. 1998). The amendment conforms the language of the Rule to its original intent, which was to impose an absolute bar on extrinsic evidence only if the sole purpose for offering the evidence was to prove the witness' character for veracity. *See* Advisory Committee Note to Rule 608(b) (stating that the Rule is "[i]n conformity with Rule 405, which forecloses use of evidence of specific incidents as proof in chief of character unless character is in issue in the case . . . .").

By limiting the application of the Rule to proof of a witness' character for truthfulness, the amendment leaves the admissibility of extrinsic evidence offered for other grounds of impeachment (such as contradiction, prior inconsistent statement, bias and mental capacity) to Rules 402 and 403. *See, e.g., United States v. Winchenbach*, 197 F.3d 548 (1st Cir. 1999) (admissibility of a prior inconsistent statement offered for impeachment is governed by Rules 402 and 403, not Rule 608(b)); *United States v. Tarantino*, 846 F.2d 1384 (D.C. Cir. 1988) (admissibility of extrinsic evidence offered to contradict a witness is governed by Rules 402 and 403); *United States v. Lindemann*, 85 F.3d 1232 (7th Cir. 1996) (admissibility of extrinsic evidence of bias is governed by Rules 402 and 403).

It should be noted that the extrinsic evidence prohibition of Rule 608(b) bars any reference to the consequences that a witness might have suffered as a result of an alleged bad act. For example, Rule 608(b) prohibits counsel from mentioning that a witness was suspended or disciplined for the conduct that is the subject of impeachment, when that conduct is offered only to prove the character of the witness. *See United States v. Davis*, 183 F.3d 231, 257, n.12 (3d Cir. 1999) (emphasizing that in attacking the defendant's character for truthfulness "the government cannot make reference to Davis's forty-four day suspension or that Internal Affairs found that he lied about" an incident because "[s]uch evidence would not only be hearsay to the extent it contains assertion of fact, it would be inadmissible extrinsic evidence under Rule 608(b)"). *See also* Stephen A. Saltzburg, *Impeaching the Witness: Prior Bad Acts and Extrinsic Evidence*, 7 Crim. Just. 28, 31 (Winter 1993) ("counsel should not be permitted to circumvent the no-extrinsic-evidence provision by tucking a third person's opinion about prior acts into a question asked of the witness who has denied the act.").

For purposes of consistency the term "credibility" has been replaced by the term "character for truthfulness" in the last sentence of subdivision (b). The term "credibility" is also used in subdivision (a). But the Committee found it unnecessary to substitute "character for truthfulness" for "credibility" in Rule 608(a), because subdivision (a)(1) already serves to limit impeachment to proof of such character.

Rules 609(a) and 610 also use the term "credibility" when the intent of those Rules is to regulate impeachment of a witness' character for truthfulness. No inference should be derived from the fact that the Committee proposed an amendment to Rule 608(b) but not to Rules 609 and 610.

### Proposed Rule 804 (b)(3). Statement Against Interest.[*]

\* \* \*

(b) Hearsay exceptions. – The following are not excluded by the hearsay rule if the declarant is unavailable as a witness:

\* \* \*

(3) Statement against interest. – A statement ~~which~~ that was at the time of its making so far contrary to the declarant's pecuniary or proprietary interest, or so far tended to subject the declarant to civil or criminal liability, or to render invalid a claim by the declarant against another, that a reasonable person in the declarant's position would not have made the statement unless believing it to be true. But a ~~A~~ statement tending to expose the declarant to criminal liability ~~and offered to exculpate the accused~~ is ~~not~~ admissible ~~unless~~ under this subdivision in the following circumstances only: (A) if offered in a civil case or to exculpate an accused in a criminal case, it is supported by corroborating circumstances that clearly indicate ~~the~~ its trustworthiness, or ~~of the statement~~ (B) if offered to inculpate an accused, it is supported by particularized guarantees of trustworthiness.

\* \* \*

---

[*]Matter to be added is underlined. Matter to be omitted is lined through. [As this Supplement went to press in June, 2002, Proposed Rule 804(b)(3) had been approved by the Standing Committee and re-submitted for public comment. Earlier public comment, particularly that of the Department of Justice, had led to changes in an earlier version of the Proposed Rule. Because the changes were substantive, the Standing Committee sought additional public comment. In the normal course of the rule-making process, the Proposed Rule cannot become law before December 1, 2004. -Eds.]

## Proposed Rule 804(b)(3)

### Advisory Committee Note (2002)

The Rule has been amended in two respects:

1) To require a showing of corroborating circumstances when a declaration against penal interest is offered in a civil case. *See, e.g., American Automotive Accessories, Inc. v. Fishman,* 175 F.3d 534, 541 (7th Cir. 1999) (requiring a showing of corroborating circumstances for a declaration against penal interest offered in a civil case).

2) To confirm the requirement that the prosecution   provide a showing of "particularized guarantees of trustworthiness" when a declaration against penal interest is offered against an accused in a criminal case. This standard is intended to assure that the exception meets constitutional requirements, and to guard against the inadvertent waiver of constitutional protections. *See Lilly v. Virginia,* 527 U.S. 116, 134-138 (1999) (holding that the hearsay exception for declarations against penal interest is not "firmly-rooted"and requiring a finding that hearsay admitted under a non-firmly-rooted exception must bear "particularized guarantees of trustworthiness" to be admissible under the Confrontation Clause).

The "particularized guarantees" requirement assumes that the court has already found that the hearsay statement is genuinely disserving of the declarant's penal interest. *See Williamson v. United States*, 512 U.S. 594, 603 (1994) (statement must be "squarely self-inculpatory" to be admissible under Rule 804(b)(3)). "Particularized guarantees" therefore must be independent from the fact that the statement tends to subject the declarant to criminal liability. The "against penal interest" factor should not be double-counted as a particularized guarantee. *See Lilly v. Virginia,* 527 U.S. at 138 (fact that statement may have been disserving to the declarant's interest does not establish particularized guarantees of trustworthiness because it "merely restates the fact that portions of his statements were technically against penal interest").

The amendment does not affect the existing requirement that the accused provide corroborating circumstances for exculpatory statements. The case law identifies some factors that may be useful to   consider   in determining whether corroborating circumstances clearly indicate the trustworthiness of the statement. Those factors include (*see, e.g.,   United States v. Hall,* 165 F.3d 1095 (7th Cir. 1999)):

(1) the timing and circumstances under which the statement was made;

(2) the declarant's motive in making the statement and whether there was a reason for the declarant to lie;

(3) whether the declarant repeated the statement and did so consistently, even under different circumstances;

(4) the party or parties to whom the statement was made;

(5) the relationship between the declarant and the opponent of the evidence; and

(6) the nature and strength of independent evidence relevant to the conduct in question.

Other factors may be pertinent under the circumstances. The credibility of the witness who relates the statement in court is not, however, a proper factor for the court to consider in assessing corroborating circumstances. To base admission or exclusion of a hearsay statement on the credibility of the witness would usurp the jury's role in assessing the credibility of testifying witnesses.

## Rejected Fed. R. Crim. Proc. 26(b)*

*Rule 26. Taking Testimony*

*(a) In General.* In every trial the testimony of witnesses must be taken in open court, unless otherwise provided by a statute or by rules adopted under 28 U.S.C. §§2072-2077.

*(b) Transmitting Testimony from a Different Location.* In the interest of justice, the court may authorize contemporaneous, two-way video presentation in open court of testimony from a witness who is at a different location if:

(1) the requesting party establishes exceptional circumstances for such transmission;

(2) appropriate safeguards for the transmission are used; and

(3) the witness is unavailable within the meaning of Federal Rule of Evidence 804(a)(4)-(5).

---

*On April 29, 2002, the Supreme Court rejected a Judicial Conference proposal to amend Rule 26 to provide for two-way-videotaped testimony. The rejected language is underlined in text. See http://a257.g.akamaitech.net/7/257/2422/29apr20021600/www.supremecourtus.gov/orders/courtorders/frcr02p_scalia.pdf (visited June 18, 2002). -Eds.